Helping Your College Student Succeed

THE
PARENT'S
CRASH
COURSE
IN
CAREER
PLANNING

Marcia B. Harris & Sharon L. Jones

The Parent's Crash Course in Career Planning:
Helping Your College Student Succeed (Revised and Expanded)

Copyright © 2007 by Marcia B. Harris & Sharon L. Jones
Published by Career Dimensions in Raleigh, NC

First Printing: 1996 by VGM Career Horizons, a division of NTC
Publishing Group

Library of Congress Control Number: 2007937137

ISBN 978-0-6151-6337-6

CONTENTS

··

About the Authors

Marcia B. Harris is a recognized authority on college career services, with over twenty-five years of experience at three different colleges and universities. She is currently director of University Career Services at The University of North Carolina at Chapel Hill. Ms. Harris has been a consultant on college career issues for over forty organizations, including IBM and Philip Morris USA; she has appeared on ABC Worldwide News with Charles Gibson and has been cited in The Wall St. Journal, Time Magazine, and The New York Times. Ms. Harris has been active in the National Association of Colleges and Employers (NACE) and is a past president of the Southeastern Association of Colleges and Employers (SACE). She is the recipient of several prestigious awards, including the SACE Ajax-Griffin Outstanding Contribution Award, the NACE/Chevron Outstanding Achievement Award for Innovation (twice), and the NACE Award of Excellence for Technical Innovation. She holds a bachelor's degree from Vassar College and a master's degree from North Carolina State University. Ms. Harris is the mother of two successfully employed college graduates.

Sharon L. Jones has career counseling and human resources experience in university, corporate, and military settings. She has advised students at the University of North Carolina at Chapel Hill for sixteen years. Through a human resources consulting firm, she worked for more than five years with the "trailing spouses" of employees transferred from major corporations. She provided these clients assistance with all facets of career exploration and the job search. Her clients' occupations were diverse, from accountant, archeology technician, and astrophysicist to e-commerce manager, graphic designer, sonographer, social worker, and toxicologist. Sharon has served as a graduate school/career advisor for *U.S. News and World Report Online*. She worked in human resources for five years in the oil industry, with responsibilities in recruiting and training. A former Army officer in personnel management, she served in Heidelberg, Germany and was promoted to captain in the Army Reserves. Ms. Jones earned an M.S. in Industrial Relations from the Krannert Graduate School of Management at Purdue University and a B.S. in Behavioral Science from Southern Colorado State College.

Foreword

··

This book has been written in response to the increasing interest among parents in helping their college-age children plan for their career. Many of today's parents realize that the job market has changed significantly from when they entered the work force. They need up-to-date information to advise their children.

As career counselors we have seen a steady growth in the number of inquiries we receive each year from parents of college students and of prospective students. They ask such questions as, "What is the best major?" "How many students find jobs after graduation?" and "What is the average starting salary of new graduates?"

While these questions are understandably on parents' minds, more appropriate questions would be, "How can my son or daughter receive help choosing the best major for his or her interests and abilities?" "What percentage of students majoring in _____ (marine science, history, etc.) is employed by graduation?" and "What is the average starting salary of new graduates entering the field of _____ (broadcasting, banking, etc.)?"

There are many additional, perhaps even more important, questions that parents should be asking, like, "Which skills are most in demand by employers?" "How can my son or daughter prepare while in college to be competitive in the marketplace upon graduation?" "Which services does the university provide to help my child plan for his or her career?" "When should these services be used?" and "Is graduate school necessary to enter the field in which my child is interested?"

The Parent's Crash Course in Career Planning answers these questions and many more. We hope that you will read it, discuss the contents with your college student both before and during college, and refer to it often.

We are firm believers that the advice within this book works; we have seen evidence of its success time and time again. We wish you and your child wonderful years of excitement, discovery, and growth during the college experience, and we wish your child satisfying employment upon graduation.

Dedication

....

To my husband, Lenny, for his constant love and support, and to my children, Todd and Stacey, for proving that the advice of this book works.

MBH

To my husband, Garry, for the inspiration to write this book, and to my parents. Lowell and Thelma Wiatt, for their love and encouragement.

SLJ

CHAPTER 1

GETTING A HEAD START: WHAT TO DO IN THE EARLY COLLEGE YEARS

"I'm Keeping My Options Open"

It was college graduation day. After the ceremony, while his sister snapped their photograph, Alec stood happily next to his parents, who were beaming with pride. Their son had just graduated from an excellent school and was starting a great job in three weeks. Not only had he been offered this job well before graduation, he had had several good job offers to choose from.

Also in the crowd of parents and new graduates was David. He, too, was excited about his graduation, as were his parents, but they all had a bit of anxiety that they were trying not to think about today. David had started applying for jobs a few months before graduation, but so far nothing had developed. His parents did not have a problem with him returning home and living with them for a while, yet they were concerned that he had no good job prospects at this time.

Why is it that whether it is a strong or weak job market, some students graduate from college with a job in hand–maybe having had two or three offers to choose from–whereas others spend months after graduation searching for employment and then have to settle for a job that is less than satisfying?

Sometimes the answer is the particular major or career field the student has selected. A field in which employees are in high demand and short supply, like pharmacy, for example, almost guarantees the new graduate employment. Most of the time, though, the difference between the student who has success in the job market versus the one who has a great deal of difficulty is due to the difference in the preparation and planning the students have given to their future career while in college.

Getting a Head Start: What to do in the Early College Years

Many students enter college with some vague idea of what they might want to do when they finish. Few of these students actually enter those fields. It is common for students to change their mind–and indeed their major–several times while in school. They may take their first organic chemistry course and realize that perhaps medical school isn't for them after all! They may enroll in anthropology and suddenly become excited about a field they barely knew existed. Or they may have a summer internship in banking and become fascinated by the financial world.

There is nothing wrong with a student's being unsure about his or her career direction for the first few years of college. The problem comes when a student puts off thinking about a career, let alone planning for it, until shortly before graduation (or even after).

Usually students avoid preparing for a career out of a combination of fear and ignorance. They are unsure of what they want to do, which is frightening, and they are unaware of the importance of preparation while in college. Often they believe that focusing on a career direction will limit their options–anathema to most college kids! So they reason that by not planning for a career, they can keep themselves open to a myriad of possibilities, which they hope will be available upon graduation.

Unfortunately, their inaction has just the opposite effect. With few exceptions, students graduating with "only" a college degree–even from a "name" school and with good grades–are not generally able to compete in today's job market. Students must take responsibility for their own employability and marketability. They cannot assume that the degree alone will enable them to meet their career goals; nor can they assume, especially at a large university, that someone from their institution will ensure that they are doing all that is necessary regarding career planning. College is like a large smorgasbord: one can choose mostly junk food and empty calories or select nutritious, well-balanced items that help build and maintain fitness. A student can go through the college experience opting for the easiest courses and spending free time partying and going to football games, or a student can choose intellectually challenging courses, participate in meaningful activities, and prepare for future career possibilities.

According to the Bureau of Labor Statistics, between 2004-2014 nearly 13.9 million college graduates will be competing for about 6.9 million "pure-college jobs," occupations in which most people hold at least a bachelor's degree. Another 7 million graduates will enter "mixed occupations," in which a four-year degree is not required. According to the University of Michigan, half of 2006 bachelor's degree recipients moved back home after graduation; 44% of 2005 graduates still lived with their parents a year later.

Employers, having such a vast supply of new graduates to choose from (almost 1.5 million a year), are becoming increasingly particular about their requirements. Whereas in the past they were primarily looking for bright, well-educated young people, today they are looking for young people who are bright and well-educated, but who also *have skills in areas of interest to them*–such as accounting or computers–*have demonstrated leadership experience, and have relevant work experience.*

You, as a parent, can do much to help your son or daughter acquire the credentials for entering a satisfying career. You will need the interest to become involved (you probably have that or you wouldn't be reading this book), the knowledge of how to help (we'll be giving you that) and the commitment to periodically discuss your child's future with him or her. (Occasional well-informed, well-intentioned "meddling" can be healthy!) Periodic discussions with your child about the future can not only help assure that important steps towards planning will be taken, but these discussions can also help maintain closeness while your young adult is undergoing the process of changing from college student to professional. With luck, your gentle reminders and questions will be appreciated. It is important not to overdo it, though and to keep in mind that your son or daughter should ultimately be making the final decision about career selection and goals.

When to Do What

Freshman Year—Easing into College Life

Freshmen have a big job–that of adjusting to college. Even if your child is a good student, self-sufficient, easy-going, and friendly, this may be the first time he or she has had to move to a new city, live in one small room with a stranger, balance a checkbook, navigate an unfamiliar campus, *and* adjust to a far greater academic workload and level of competition than ever before. This is not the best time to bring up career planning! Most freshmen have so much going on in their lives that the vast majority are simply not receptive to planning far into the future. Some are simply not developmentally ready to take on this task.

Students should spend the first year acclimating to campus life and college-level coursework. Some find the first year, particularly the first semester, quite easy academically. They are often the students who have had an excellent secondary school preparation and have entered college with advanced credit. They may even comment that their courses are "a review of high school material." These students may have great grades in their first semester, despite lackadaisical study habits. They assume that subsequent semesters will be just as easy, and then find to their dismay that their grades steadily slide as the courses get harder.

Other students don't know what hit them that first semester. If they haven't had a strong high school preparation or did not face much competition from their peers, they will soon find that the course work and faculty expectations about performance are far greater than they have ever had to deal with. Their grades may be abysmal the first semester, which will be discouraging to them (as well as to you). Still others simply do not care about grades once they have been admitted to college, which has been their primary goal to date. They naively think that grades no longer matter.

By their senior year, though, if not earlier, students realize that their college grades do matter. Whether they are applying for admission to graduate or professional school or for a job, their academic performance is likely to be scrutinized and may very well determine whether or not they are considered.

Most students, with effort and possibly academic support from their school, can recover from one bad semester–especially if it is their first one. Rarely, though, can a student who has had two years of poor grades bring them up to a competitive level by their senior year. (A competitive level would mean a grade point average–or GPA–of about 3.0 on a 4.0 scale for most career fields. But this could be significantly higher for some other fields or for graduate or professional school admission.) Good grades, especially for freshmen, require a major commitment of time and effort. A study by the University of Iowa found that freshmen who studied four or more hours a day had average GPA's of 3.0, while those who studied less than one hour a day averaged 2.6.

So encourage your son or daughter to make grades a top priority from the beginning. Students who start out investing the time and effort to make good grades develop habits and skills that serve them well throughout college.

Freshmen should begin establishing good relationships with their academic adviser and faculty members, especially those in fields that interest them. These individuals can provide excellent career and academic advice and can serve as references for part-time jobs, internships and eventually full-time positions. Often faculty and advisors are eager to get to

4

know students on an individual basis but expect the student to take the initiative by scheduling appointments or staying after class to talk.

The freshman year is also a time for students to become involved in at least one extracurricular activity. Virtually every campus has a large variety of clubs and organizations, as well as other opportunities for students to engage in activities that interest them. Does your son enjoy writing? He can volunteer to write for the campus newspaper or other campus publications. Does your daughter have an interest in computers? She can sign up for the computer science club. Does he like to help others? He can volunteer for the Big Buddy Program. Does she want to explore business opportunities? She can join the Business Student Association.

Generally there will be an activity for almost any interest a student has. And if there isn't one, the student always has the option of forming a new organization, which is usually quite easy to do. Becoming involved in campus life, whether through student government, the residence hall, the drama club, ski team, or a fraternity or sorority, will help your child find a niche and develop a feeling of belonging. This is critical to adjustment to college and is a major factor in a student's staying in school and in being satisfied with college life.

As we will discuss later, extracurricular activities are one of the best ways to explore career interests, obtain leadership experience, and acquire skills, such as public speaking, writing, budgeting, and organizing, that are important in entering and succeeding in a career.

Students should use their summers constructively. Although it is unlikely that most freshmen will be able to obtain an internship, they may be able to work in a field of interest to them, although it will probably be at a low level.

If they have an interest in banking, they can work as a teller; if they want to explore retailing, they can work as a sales assistant in a department store; if they want exposure to the work of a veterinarian, they may be able to do clerical work in a veterinary clinic; if they want to work with children, they can be a summer camp counselor. Any type of hands-on experience will be helpful and good for the résumé later.

Other worthwhile summer activities for freshmen are study abroad, travel, volunteer work, and summer school (to bring up grades, take courses they may not be able to get into during the school year, or build credit hours in order to be able to take a lighter load some time in the future).

Time for Career Planning

Assuming that a student has made the transition to college life and is handling it fairly well, the sophomore year is typically the time to begin career planning.

What exactly is career planning? For college students, career planning involves assessing their interests, skills, abilities, and work values; deciding, either generally or specifically, what it is they want to do in life (or at least for the first few years after college); learning about the qualifications necessary to enter their desired field; and - during the next two to three years - obtaining these qualifications as well as other "enhancers" in order to be a strong candidate to compete for positions in their chosen career.

Five Steps to Career Planning

1.   Self-Assessment

As the first step to choosing a career, your child should assess his or her interests, skills, abilities and work values. Every college can provide help with this process. The campus counseling center or career office offers interest and personality inventories, which can be a good starting point. Interest inventories, or "tests," such as the Strong Interest Inventory and The Self-Directed Search, can help students assess their likes and dislikes and also measure the similarity of their likes and dislikes to those of successful workers in various occupations. (Research indicates that having similar interests to those successfully employed in a career field is likely to result in satisfaction with that field.) Personality tests, such as the Myers-Briggs Type Indicator, also provide useful data. Many career or counseling centers offer computerized guidance programs like DISCOVER and FOCUS, which students enjoy taking and find helpful. The Internet also offers free interest tests for students (one of the best is Career Key: www.careerkey.org/) and many sites to explore career fields, some with video   clips   of   people   who   work   in   various   occupations: www.jobprofiles.org/ and apps.collegeboard.com/myroad/navigator.jsp

No "test" exists, though, that can tell your son or daughter precisely what he or she should do with his or her life. Nor are there many tests that measure aptitude - what a person is good at. (Generally grades and college entrance tests like the SAT or ACT are fairly good indicators of how strong a student is in verbal and quantitative disciplines. This information can be useful when considering careers that require rigorous academic training.)

Interest and personality inventories primarily help identify patterns of an individual's interests and suggest occupations that might fit these patterns. Through further discussions with a career counselor, your son or daughter can begin to form ideas about occupations that might suit his or her values, abilities, and interests. It is important not to overlook lifestyle and working conditions issues, which include income level, working hours, work attire, prestige of position, and work environment, among others. Although these factors should not unduly influence career choice, they certainly must be considered.

Some colleges offer a career planning course for academic credit. This type of course is especially useful for freshmen or sophomores who are unsure about their major or career. Taking a career planning course is also an excellent way to ensure that at least a minimum amount of planning for the future will be done in college, since it imposes some structure and requirements upon students who, like so many of us, may be prone to procrastination.

2. Research and Exploration

The next step involves exploring possible occupations. Unfortunately, many college students choose a major or a career direction based on very little information. For instance, law school admissions offices have experienced a tremendous surge of interest in law as a result of the popularity of TV shows like "L.A. Law" and "Law and Order." Students decide to be lawyers based on their fascination with the glamour of expensive suits, glitzy offices, and unusual law cases! But many of them sadly learn that for most lawyers, the reality of practicing law bears little resemblance to how it is portrayed on television.

Students can explore careers that interest them a number of ways: reading, talking to those practicing or knowledgeable about the career, and exposure to the actual working environment.

Reading and Viewing Information

It is often said that students spend more time looking for an apartment than researching a career. Time and energy put into obtaining as much career information as possible from a variety of sources will be well worth it.

Books, professional journals, and videotapes are important and valuable sources of career information. The career office and the campus library will have these resources. Encourage your son or daughter to read a variety of materials to get different opinions and perspectives. *The Occupational Outlook Handbook*, published bi-annually by the US Department of Labor and available at www.bls.gov/oco/, gives an overview of almost every career field a college student is likely to be considering. It also includes sources to contact for further information.

There is a wealth of career information available on the Internet, including sites such as the following:

Job Profiles: www.jobprofiles.org/index.htm

US Department of Labor's Career Guide to Industries: www.jobprofiles.org/index.htm

Career Overview: www.careeroverview.com/

Alfred P. Sloan Foundation's Career Cornerstone (for careers in science, math, and technology): www.careercornerstone.org

ArtJobs: www.artjob.org

Good Works (social change organizations): goodworksfirst.org/

Talking to Others

Encourage your child to talk to people who are doing the kind of work that interests him or her. You may know someone working in the field or, through contacts, may be able to find someone who does. If not, have your child ask the career center or faculty members for names of alumni or other contacts. Another possibility is to look into professional associations related to the field and write for information and local contact names. Many of these associations have student chapters on campus or allow students to attend local meetings - a great way to gain information and also start developing a network of contacts. Many professional associations also offer scholarships and internships to student members. If your child has an interest in personnel work (now usually called human resources), he or she should check to see if there is a campus student chapter of the Society for Human Resource Management. Other examples of professional associations with student chapters are the Society of Women Engineers and the American Marketing Association. Books such as *The Occupational Outlook Handbook* or *The Encyclopedia of Associations*, available in the college library or career center, have information about relevant professional associations. Local service organizations like the Rotary Club or Civitans may also be helpful.

Students should conduct "information interviews" once they have located contacts in fields of interest to them. Unlike a job interview, an information interview is conducted by the student (as opposed to the employer) and, as the name implies, is for informational purposes only. Most people love talking with others about what they do, and most professionals especially enjoy giving advice to students. The career center can coach your son or daughter on how to locate contacts and approach them to request an information interview, how to develop a list of questions to ask, and how to actually conduct the interview. It is important to always send a thank-you letter within a week, and the smart student will stay in touch from time to time to retain the contact.

Colleges offer numerous other ways for underclassmen to begin making contacts with and learning from employers. Most schools hold career fairs and other career-related programs, such as career panels, employer presentations, and graduate/professional school days. Sophomores and juniors (and interested freshmen) should attend these programs and ask questions about entry-level requirements and desired qualifications. Students should use these events to begin getting to know employers and using them as resources. A student who has an interest in a career in consumer sales, for example, can start preparing for it by asking Black and Decker or General Mills recruiters at a campus career fair for advice on a major, coursework, part-time or summer work experience, and extracurricular activities. Even with the hundreds - and sometimes thousands - of students these recruiters meet on the many campuses they visit, they often remember the assertive student who has talked with them each year starting as a freshman or sophomore. By the time that student is a senior and ready to seek a job, he or she is known to the recruiter and has an edge over other students who are starting from scratch.

3.   Gaining Experience

Since the freshman year is primarily spent adjusting to college and the senior year either looking for a job or applying to graduate school (or possibly both), a student has basically only two years to make himself the best possible candidate for obtaining his goal upon graduation. Whether that goal is an entry-level job or admission to graduate or professional school, it is essential for the student to maximize opportunities during the sophomore and junior years to acquire the credentials that will give an advantage over the many other applicants competing for the same goal.

Extracurricular Activities

We've already discussed the value of participation in extracurricular activities. Not only do these activities help students make friends and find a place of belonging, but they also provide opportunities for learning about careers and for developing and demonstrating many skills.

Almost every employer hiring new college graduates seeks students with both leadership and teamwork skills. How do students acquire and demonstrate these skills? Usually through involvement in student government, their sorority or fraternity, the residence hall, athletics, or campus organizations. Students may also participate in activities off-campus, such as religious, community service, or political groups. Some community organizations, such as non-profits, want student representation on their boards. Students must bear in mind, however, that it may take several years to grow into and earn significant leadership positions.

Some students join so many organizations that they spread themselves too thin. Their grades may suffer, and they may find themselves feeling very stressed. Generally it is advisable for a student to be involved in no more than three extracurricular activities (fewer in their first year or two), and to try to have substantial leadership roles in the activities they select.

Experience

Years ago college seniors bemoaned the catch-22 of getting experience. "Every employer," they would say, "wants to hire someone with experience. How can you ever get experience if no one will hire you without it?" Today that is not a valid complaint. There are numerous ways for students to obtain relevant work experience while still in school.

Field Experience/Co-Operative Education

Students—and their parents—must realize that obtaining marketable skills and career-related experience is a critical part of their education. For some majors experience will be built into the curriculum. Education majors, for example, do student teaching, so they graduate with experience in their field. Nursing, pharmacy, and most health-related majors have "clinical rotations" in hospitals or other appropriate work settings. Many technical majors, like engineering or computer science, are either required or have the option to participate in cooperative education programs and thus have a significant amount of experience upon graduation.

Cooperative education is an academic program that alternates periods of study on campus with periods of career-related work experience off-campus. For example, a student studying electrical engineering may be a full-time student on campus in the fall semester, then work full-time for an employer like IBM in the spring semester (off-campus, but obtaining course credit for the work experience), and then return to campus full-time in the summer or the next fall. Generally a student involved in a cooperative education program (usually called co-op) will have two to three work experiences, often with the same employer. Co-op allows the student to test out a career, make contacts, and obtain work experience. Additionally, co-op experience almost always is paid and carries academic credit. It is an ideal way to blend academic and work experience. The only possible drawback is that it usually extends graduation to at least five years. Co-op programs are almost always available to students in technical programs like engineering, and may be available to others, depending on the college or university. It may also be possible for students attending colleges without a cooperative education program to create a similar type of experience with the help of the career or internship office.

Part-time Jobs, Volunteer Work, and Internships

Students in most majors do not have a ready-made path to obtain experience. But there are many ways for them to do so through part-time jobs, volunteer work, and internships. All else being equal, many employers favor the candidate who has held a part-time job while in school. As a recruiter from Nissan Motors stated, "Working part-time–even at an unrelated job–demonstrates industriousness, organizational skills, and a knowledge of the expectations of the working world."

Part-time jobs are available both on campus and with employers in college communities. Students might need to be creative in finding them, though. Encourage your child to check the website of their career office and financial aid office for job listings and to read the classified ads in the campus and local newspapers. Directly approaching campus departments, faculty members, and local employers may also result in part-time work. The biology or chemistry department is a natural place for a student wishing to get lab experience to look. But that same student might not think about contacting the university medical, dental or veterinary school, local hospitals, health care clinics, pharmaceutical firms, or drug testing companies. Likewise, in addition to the campus IT (information technology) or computer science department, a student wanting to acquire computer skills might check with the library, the accounting office, or even the career center - all of which use computers and usually need more expertise in this area.

In addition to part-time jobs, students may volunteer to work unpaid in exchange for training and experience. In some fields it is very difficult for students to find paid positions. This is especially true in the arts, broadcasting, entertainment, journalism, museum work, government and politics, anthropology and other fields that are not in high demand. Although it may be hard for you, and your son or daughter, to accept the fact that he or she may have to work "for free," if you consider this as another part of the total educational experience, it may be easier to swallow. (At least you're not paying tuition for it!)

Many colleges now offer service-learning courses, which allow students to combine academic credit courses with applied, hands-on work in the community. This is a way for students interested in non-profit, research, government, and social service work to gain experience.

What exactly is an internship? The definition may differ from campus to campus, but the common thread among internships is that they are career-related learning experiences. Beyond that they may vary significantly. They may be paid or unpaid, be full-time or part-time, take place during the summer or the school year, and carry academic credit or not. More information on internships will be provided in Chapter 5.

4.   Developing Marketable Skills and Enhancers

Most employers today are less interested in a student's major than in the student's skills. A prominent management consultant was quoted in *Fortune* magazine as saying, "Special skills and abilities have moved from being the way to win to being the price of admission."

Although some fields, like engineering, nursing, or pharmacy, virtually require a degree in a specific major in order to enter them, for most fields it is the candidate's skills and abilities that will determine whether he or she gets the job and is successful at it. This should be good news for college students. The major then takes on less importance. Knowing that they can acquire skills and experiences that employers seek through a variety of ways, there is less pressure to choose the "right" major.

What are the skills that employers most frequently seek in new graduates? Obviously, these will differ depending on the particular field and job, but employers most often request the following skills:

- Quantitative skills (e.g., accounting, statistics, economics)
- Communication skills (written and oral)
- Marketing skills (selling, persuading)
- Computer skills (programming/software development, network administration, web design)
- Scientific skills (laboratory, research)
- Foreign language skills (especially Spanish, Chinese, Arabic, Farsi, and Portuguese)
- Leadership and teamwork skills

Since few individuals can excel in all of these areas, encourage your son or daughter to choose at least two or three of them to develop as strengths. These skills can be acquired through coursework, volunteer or paid work, extracurricular activities, and other experiences such as studying or living abroad.

The Concept Of Enhancers

The job market, like other economic markets, is based on supply and demand. The greater the supply of workers in a particular field in relation to the demand for those workers, the greater the difficulty in finding work in that field. Conversely, the greater the demand for workers in a field in relation to the supply of them, the easier to find work in that field. Let's look at two fields: broadcasting and mathematics teaching. Broadcasting is a very difficult field to enter because of the large supply of individuals wanting to enter it relative to the number of job openings. On the other hand, high school math teachers are in short supply; therefore, someone graduating with a degree in secondary mathematics education should not have much difficulty finding employment.

An individual may bring some "extras" in addition to the degree, which we call enhancers, to his or her candidacy. A student graduating from college with a basic liberal arts degree and little more is not likely to easily find a job in broadcasting. That student needs as many enhancers as he or she can possibly obtain.

What might these enhancers be? For the field of broadcasting, a list of desirable enhancers might look like this:

- Course work or major in radio or television or broadcasting
- Good grades
- Part-time job at the campus radio station
- Summer internships at a radio or television station
- Involvement in the campus student broadcasting association

It is important that as your son or daughter begins to focus on a career direction, he or she consider the supply-demand ratio for workers. The greater the supply of workers relative to the demand for them, the greater the need for enhancers. Fields for which enhancers are especially important are the arts, entertainment, social services, communications/broadcasting, museum work, and historical preservation.

How to Gain Marketable Skills

- Required//Elective Cources
- Student Organizations/Activities
- Volunteer Work
- Jobs (part-time, summer, work-study, and self-employment)
- Internships

ENHANCERS

- Extracurricular Activities
- Contacts
- Job-Relevant Skills
- Grades
- Job-Seeking Skills
- Relevant Course Work
- Work Experience/ Internships

5.   Learning Job-Seeking Skills

Although many students think they can wait until their senior year to begin learning how to write a résumé, interview, and search for a job, these skills are important to underclassmen who will be applying for internships and part-time jobs.

We recommend that sophomores and juniors register and begin using the career office for career exploration and planning and for job search techniques.

Developing A Career Plan

Encourage your child to develop a career plan as a sophomore and to review it each year, making adjustments as necessary. The plan includes a list of projected activities, experiences, and skills to develop for the next two years along with an action plan indicating how the student will work towards it through their college years.

Todd was a student who enjoyed his English courses but wasn't sure about a career direction. He was considering several options such as writing, teaching, and public relations. He decided to major in English, since he thought he could do best in a subject he liked, but wanted to plan for a broad number of career possibilities upon graduation. The career plan he developed with the help of a career planning counselor in his college career office looked like this:

CAREER PLAN FOR TODD

Sophomore Year:

- Declare English as a major
- Write for the school newspaper
- Volunteer for the campus Big Buddy program
- Take elective courses in public speaking & business communications
- Join the student chapter of the Public Relations Society of America
- Research and make contacts in public relations, advertising, writing, and publishing
- Seek help from career office on résumé-writing and interviewing
- Get a summer job (or unpaid internship) in a public relations or advertising firm

---

Junior Year:

- Take elective courses in computer skills (to learn spreadsheet, desktop publishing, web design and graphics software)
- Continue to write for the campus newspaper; seek assistant editor position
- Work as a tutor for students having difficulty in English courses
- Take additional elective courses in public relations, advertising, and accounting (to acquire a valuable marketable skill)
- Do a course project related to a real-world public relations problem
- Run for office in the campus public relations club
- Get a summer internship in a public relations firm
- Regularly read professional trade journals related to public relations and advertising (such as *O'Dwyers Public Relations News* or *Advertising Age*).

By the time Todd was a senior, he had decided upon a career in public relations. Through the development and implementation of his career plan, he was in a strong position to fulfill his goal of finding an entry-level position in his chosen field. Had he decided to pursue some of his other interests, like publishing or teaching, he also would have strong credentials. (For a teaching career, though, he most likely would have to obtain certification or an additional degree–although there are some avenues to teach without either of these.)

A career plan will help your child better organize his or her time and be aware of what must be done over the sophomore and junior years to explore and prepare for career options. Like most of us, students are more likely to follow-through on good intentions if they have a written plan of action with specific tasks and timetables. At the end of this chapter is a worksheet for a career plan which you and your son or daughter can work on together. We suggest that your child discuss the plan with a college career counselor.

At least one college has created a program guaranteeing that students in certain curricula will have a job with a competitive salary within ninety days of graduation or the college will provide up to 36 additional undergraduate credits tuition-free while students continue their job search.

To be eligible for the plan, students must agree to complete a bachelor's degree with a 2.75 grade point average, be actively involved with a campus organization, complete a college-sponsored work experience (co-op or its equivalent), attend annual Career Day activities, attend at least three career seminars, actively work with the career services office and make a good faith effort to find a job after graduation. As Tom, one student considering attending this college, said, "If I want to get a good job, I've got to do this stuff anyway."

Tom is right. Colleges don't need to offer guarantees and students don't need to sign agreements. A student who wants to find a good job has to do "this stuff," and one who does is very likely to find a good job within three months of graduation, guarantee or no guarantee.

CAREER PLAN WORKSHEET

Sophomore Year

- Elective courses to develop marketable skills:

  _____

  _____

- Extracurricular activities to investigate/participate in:

  _____

- Career areas to explore:

  _____

- Information interviews to conduct:

  _____

- Seek help from counseling center or career office with:

- Part-time job:

  _____

- Apply for summer job or internship with:

  _____

  _____

- Other:

  _____

Junior Year:

- Major:

  _____

- Elective courses to enhance major/develop marketable skills:

  _____

  _____

- Extracurricular /volunteer activities and leadership roles:

  _____

- Information interviews:

  _____

- Part-time work:

  _____

- Seek co-op or internship with:

  _____

- Seek assistance from career office with:

  _____

- Other (may include graduate/professional school investigation; admissions test preparation):

Summary

··

Timetable For Career Planning

Freshman Year

- Acclimate to college life
- Concentrate on making good grades
- Become involved in extra-curricular activities

Sophomore and Junior Years

- Assess interests through testing
- Research careers of possible interest through reading and talking with those in the field
- Attend career days and other career-related programs sponsored by the campus career office
- Intensify involvement in extra-curricular activities and assume at least one leadership position

- Gain career-related experience through volunteer work or extracurricular activities

- Obtain summer or part-time career-related work experience through paid or unpaid jobs and internships

- Develop marketable skills

- Build enhancers

- Develop a career plan

- Read professional trade journals in fields of interest (many are free online)

- Seek assistance from the career office with career planning, interviewing, and résumé writing

- Prepare for graduate/professional school, if appropriate

Marketable Skills

Develop strength in at least two or three of the following areas:

- Quantitative skills

- Communication skills

- Marketing skills

- Computer skills

- Scientific skills

- Foreign language skills

- Leadership teamwork skills

Gain marketable skills through required/elective/service learning courses:

- Student organizations/activities

- Volunteer work

- Internships

- Jobs (part-time, summer, work-study, self-employment)
- Study abroad (for language and cross-cultural skills)

Enhancers

- Grades

- Extracurricular activities

- Contacts

- Marketable skills

- Job-seeking skills

- Relevant coursework/ course projects

- Work experience/internships

Conversation Starters for Parents and Students

....

1. Which campus activities do you think would interest you? Have you looked into joining them?

2. Which services does your career office offer to help students select a major or make career decisions?

3. Which summer jobs or internships do you think might be available to someone with your interests or major? Have you checked with the career office about how to obtain them?

4. Let's think about people we know in the fields that interest you (such as neighbors or relatives) so you can set up informational interviews with them.

5. Are you planning to attend career programs offered on campus? (If not, why not?)

6. Have you sought help from the career office on a career plan?

CHAPTER 2

STARTING OUT: FIRST JOBS FOR NEW GRADS (INCLUDING "HOT" CAREERS)

Lulu is an innovative, quirky venture—a rigorous, challenging environment where every day we have to be better than we have ever been and do it even better tomorrow. We are seeking smart, creative, energetic, web-savvy "lulus" for various positions. Think you're a good fit? Take the quiz...!

Lulu Quiz

Internationalization:

Have you studied or lived abroad and loved it? (+1)

Are you multilingual? (+2)

Accomplishments:

Do you do something better than anyone else? Tell us what. (+1)

Have you achieved something great? (+1)

Do you possess remarkable intelligence and yet you're still humble? (+2)

Renaissance skill set:

Calling all Musicians, Thespians, Orators, Artisans, Videographers, and Bloggers - creativity in any area! (+1 each)

Sense of Humor (+1), **Flexibility** (+1), **Non-traditional thought patterns** (+2)

Convince us of your score!

Lulu, a fast-growing North Carolina technology firm and independent publisher, is looking for special employees. Like many employers, the company does not recruit any particular college major, but describes its culture and ideal applicants through its website.

Who would have guessed a decade ago that consumers would buy screensavers for their personal computers, music downloads for i-pods, ringtones for mobile phones, and GPS equipment for their automobiles? Who would have expected criminologists to develop geographic profiling techniques to track serial killers or that surgeons would use robotics to increase their precision?

New and emerging occupations are appearing on job boards and in classified ads, mystifying many job seekers. They think, "What is an information architect? A resettlement coordinator? A customer insight analyst? A creative fragrance associate?" These new types of opportunities are likely to be multidisciplinary, that is requiring skills and study in several different areas.

Because of a rapidly changing workplace, college students need to prepare themselves in a different way than those who came before them. What kind of background is likely to be advantageous?

- A strong liberal arts education with interdisciplinary skills, or training in an area in particular demand
- Experience related to the student's career objective through internships, part-time jobs, or volunteer work
- Proficiency in a foreign language (especially Chinese, Spanish, or Arabic)
- A global perspective and cross-cultural awareness (e.g. study abroad, international studies courses)
- Leadership and teamwork skills through extracurricular activities, volunteer work, group study projects, or work experience
- Strong communication skills: writing, interpersonal, and public speaking
- Personality traits such as adaptability, initiative, creativity, and persuasiveness

An ancient Chinese curse says, "May you live in interesting times." The pace of change will make these unpredictable years! Your child should choose a career direction that utilizes his or her strengths and matches his or her values and interests. Even if the job market undergoes unexpected changes, your child will have established a solid foundation for future career moves.

Students and Career Choice

According to the Annual Freshman Survey by the Cooperative Institutional Research Program, the top three reasons college freshmen give for attending college are "to learn more about things that interest me," "to get a better job" and "to make more money." Ironically, many students do not make the most of their college years to target a career and prepare for employment. They take the "Scarlett O'Hara" approach to career choices—"I'll think about it tomorrow." Other students (and often, parents) believe the common myth, "You can no longer get a good job with just a bachelor's degree." They decide to focus their energies on graduate school applications and overlook many attractive job opportunities that do not require further education. Even when students do explore career options, they often take a one-dimensional approach. They ask, "What are the highest paying jobs?" or "What are the jobs that have the fastest growth?" As a result, some make decisions without regard to their natural abilities or sincere interests.

A student's evaluation of career options may also be affected by peer pressure. Some students allow others (e.g., classmates, parents, or faculty) to unduly influence the process. Graduates often express regret at allowing themselves to be talked into (or out of) a career field. A student should ultimately make career decisions based on sound self-analysis as well as on field of interest.

Students sometimes avoid making a career choice because they are afraid of making the wrong decision, as if a career focus can never be changed. But members of Generation Y are expected to change careers (not just jobs) an average of three or four times. So a first job does not signify a lifetime commitment but rather a starting point.

How Parents Can Help with Career Decision-Making

Your child may turn to you for career advice; however, it's difficult to keep up with job trends outside your own industry or occupation. This quiz may help you determine how much you know about the most recent changes in the workplace.

HOW MUCH DO YOU KNOW ABOUT THE JOB MARKET?

1. Which of these health occupations is not in high demand?

   a) Nurse b) Physician Assistant c) Dietician d) Food Technologist

2. Which subjects have such a shortage of licensed teachers that many public schools will consider applicants who have majored in the subject but lack a teaching certificate?

   a) Mathematics b) Science c) Foreign Language d) All

3. What percentage of federal government jobs are located in Washington, D.C.?

   a) 75 % b) 60 % c) 40% d)15 %

4 According to a survey of employers recruiting college graduates, which is true?

   a) Students with multiple majors are more competitive for jobs.

   b) Study abroad provides students with a big advantage in the job search.

   c) The best experience on a student's résumé is a career-related internship.

   d) A graduate degree ensures higher competitiveness and starting salary.

5. According to the National Association of Colleges and Employers, which "soft skill" is most valued by employers?

   a) Teamwork b) Communications c) Interpersonal d) Creativity

6. It's always an advantage for a student to use credits from passed AP tests.

   a) True b) False

7. The most marketable foreign language is:

   a) Spanish b) German c) Japanese d) Chinese

8. What are recruiters likely to look for on a student's résumé to identify leadership skills?

    a) Supervising others, such as a job as head waiter or senior camp counselor

    b) Starting a business, such as lawn mowing or e-bay sales

    c) A responsible elected position as an officer in a student club on campus

    d) Initiating and completing an independent study project

9. A liberal arts major (i.e. English, History, Psychology) is generally not marketable

    a) True   b) False

10. What percentage of students in the U.S. have completed an internship by graduation?

    a) 20%   b) 40%   c) 50%   d) 60%

    Check how you did on page 52.

An *Occupational Outlook Quarterly* article about career myths cautions those exploring careers to expand their options rather than eliminate possible choices based on unfounded assumptions. Parents often have misconceptions about careers. If your child wants to major in art, what is your first impression? You are probably concerned about whether she can support herself and suggest a more "practical" major. However, artists are employed as graphic designers, website designers, medical photographers or illustrators, and computer game animators. Does library science sound dull? Perhaps you haven't heard about information brokers, search engine analysts, knowledge management consultants, or ontologists.

How can you help your child explore different career options? First, consider these questions:

- "What are my child's natural abilities--in what does he or she excel?"

- "Which types of activities motivate my child to do his or her best? When do I see sparks of passion and excitement?"
- "What are job trends related to my child's career interests?"

You want your child to be happy and successful in work. Ideally, your child will choose a career that is consistent with his or her strengths and abilities. However, students may have trouble being objective about their potential for different careers. As one said, "I want to be realistic, but I don't want to sell myself short either."

Outstanding performers bring something extra to their jobs, perhaps through extraordinary effort, resourcefulness, or creativity. Parents can help their children identify what motivates them to go the extra mile, so that they are more likely to choose work at which they have a greater chance to succeed. Which of your child's accomplishments is he or she most proud of? How does he or she spend free time?

Glamour Fields

After targeting some career fields for exploration, your child may be tempted to make a choice that is based on limited information. One career field may offer high salaries for new graduates but have such rigorous requirements that successful candidates must have nearly a straight-A average. The job may also require frequent travel or relocation, long hours, and stressful working conditions. Another field that sounds glamorous or adventurous may offer low compensation. A new graduate can expect to make sacrifices or trade-offs when selecting a first job after college. A career that sounds dull and routine may introduce new entrants to jobs with variety and challenge. College career counselors are a good source for information about job trends.

Students may feel peer pressure to apply for jobs that are perceived as elite and extremely competitive, such as investment banking or consulting analyst, or which are creative. Industries or fields that sound attractive to many students may be especially difficult to enter, often requiring internships (frequently unpaid) and entry level jobs at low starting salaries.

Starting Out: Entry-Level Jobs

··

There is a general misconception that there are no good jobs for students with an undergraduate degree. However, there are many options for new bachelor's-level graduates. Tables 2.1-2.8 at the end of this chapter provide an overview of typical job titles, starting compensation, predicted job growth, and majors considered for entry-level jobs. With proper preparation, college graduates in any major have diverse job opportunities.

Hot Careers

··

A "hot" job is right for your child only if he or she has the aptitude, interest, and motivation to prepare for the opportunity. The highest growth career areas for 2004-2014 include healthcare, computer science, education, and accounting/auditing.

Here is a list of careers in which there is strong job market demand and higher than average salaries, with educational level indicated:

UNDERGRADUATE DEGREE USUALLY REQUIRED	
Consulting	Business analyst
Investment Banking	Financial analyst, trader, stock analyst
Business	Actuary, marketing research analyst, web marketer
Computer Science	Software engineer, systems analyst, computer security specialist, usability engineer, database administrator
Health	Nurse, biostatistician, diagnostic medical sonographer, health information administrator, clinical research associate, dental hygienist, nutritionist, health physicist
Education	Instructional designer, curriculum developer

Science/Engineering	Biomedical engineer, computer engineer, environmental engineer, electrical engineer, mechanical engineer
Decision Sciences	Risk analyst, operations research analyst

GRADUATE OR PROFESSIONAL DEGREE USUALLY REQUIRED	
Accounting	Accountant, auditor (CPA required)
Architecture	Architect
Decision Science	Risk and decision scientist
Health	Physician, pharmacist, physician's assistant, nurse practitioner, physical therapist, nurse anesthetist, occupational therapist, respiratory therapist, orthoptist (diagnoses and treats eye disorders)
Science/Technology	Biochemist, biophysicist, computer engineer
Library Science	Librarian, knowledge management analyst, information architect
Law	Lawyer
Education	Educational diagnostician (helps individualize education for special needs children); educational measurement researcher, school counselor
Linguistics	Computational linguist, knowledge engineer, ontologist

Potential for Self-employment

At least one course in entrepreneurship is offered by 2,100 colleges and universities, making it the fastest-growing discipline. If your child has an independent or entrepreneurial nature, many health and computer-related careers can be performed through telecommuting, freelancing, and obtaining contract work. Some examples of occupations to explore:

OCCUPATIONS WITH MANY ENTREPRENEURS

Architect	Patent agent
Consulting actuary	Physical therapist
Dentist	Physican
Financial adviser	Psychologist
Graphic artist	Realtor
Information broker	Social worker
Lawyer	Software engineer
Medical illustrator	Speech pathologist
Nutritionist	Technical writer
Occupational therapist	Translator/Interpreter
Optician	Web designer

A new college graduate can typically qualify for many jobs with any major.

ENTRY-LEVEL JOBS FOR ANY MAJOR

FINANCIAL	
Consumer Banking	Management trainee (branch management, lending, credit, or operations)
Investment Banking	Financial analyst, assistant trader
Securities	Stockbroker trainee
Insurance	Underwriter, claims adjuster, customer service representative
Risk analysis	Risk assessor, risk management advisor, risk analyst

Real estate	Leasing agent, financial analyst, management trainee (sales, construction, customer relations, land development)
Purchasing	Purchasing agent, contract specialist
RESEARCH (NON-SCIENCE)	Business analyst, research associate, research assistant
JOURNALISM/RADIO/ TV/FILM	Reporter, assistant copywriter, production assistant
DIGITAL MEDIA/ARTS	Flash designer (animation), digital artist, graphic designer, illustrator, assistant Internet editor, set and exhibit designer
GOVERNMENT	Legislative assistant, special agent, inspector, regulatory analyst, program specialist
NONPROFIT	Membership representative, grant writer, fundraiser, research assistant, program assistant, writer, editor, event planning coordinator, coordinator of volunteers
HOSPITALITY	Hotel management trainee, restaurant management trainee, event planner
LAW-RELATED	Paralegal or legal researcher, probation officer
CONSULTING	Business analyst, research assistant, research associate, research analyst, associate consultant
EDUCATION	Teacher in public schools (subjects with shortage of qualified applicants), private schools (middle and secondary subjects), wilderness schools (for troubled youth)
HEALTHCARE	Clinical monitor

Although any major may qualify for numerous entry-level jobs, a student should target a few career fields and obtain related experience, college courses (such as electives or a minor), and skills to increase their chances of being hired.

Even unrelated experience can help differentiate some students from other job applicants. The CEO of Booz Allen Hamilton told *US News & World Report* that his company values "people with passion" and "cutting edge skills." He also commented that:

....

"When you find a person has run in a marathon, or they sing in an opera, or they like to climb mountains—things that challenge you as an individual to be better and do better—we find those kinds of people tend to have great success here."

....

Entry-level Job Growth

According to the U.S. Bureau of Labor Statistics, the fastest entry level growth is expected in jobs related to computer science or health.

10 FASTEST GROWING OCCUPATIONS FOR COLLEGE GRADS (2005-2025)	
Network systems and data communications analysts	55%
Physician assistants	50%
Computer software engineers	48%
Physical therapist assistants	44%
Dental hygienists	43%
Computer software engineers	43%
Network and computer systems administrators	38%
Database administrators	38%
Physical therapists	37%
Forensic science technicians	36%

Good Jobs For Undergraduates

....

Education/Social Services

According to the National Assessment of Education Progress (NAEP), proficiency levels of American students in math and science are poor. The projected number of openings for high school math and science teachers is 200,000 in the next 10 years.

An increase in the number of children qualifying for special education services, the pressure of demonstrating their progress through standardized testing, and high burnout rate of special education teachers have led to a projection of 200,000 vacancies in this field by 2010.

Public school enrollment includes over 10% of students for whom English is their second language. As a result of growing awareness of the global economy, demand has increased for classes such as Chinese and Arabic. Strong demand exists for teachers in foreign languages and bilingual education.

States and school systems are developing alternative certification programs to fill teacher openings. Some examples of these options for non-education majors include Teach Kentucky, Milwaukee and Metropolitan Multicultural Teacher Education Program, and New York City Teaching Fellows. Teach for America, a non-profit, has recruited more than 8,000 students, most of them recent liberal arts graduates, for jobs in rural and inner city locations. (See Chapter 7.)

Private or independent schools do not require teachers to be certified; they would rather hire graduates who excel (a GPA of 3.2-3.5+) in a major that is taught at the middle or high school level and can convey passion about their subject. A teaching license is not required to qualify for a youth counselor job in a wilderness education program. Preferred majors for these jobs include sociology, criminology, psychology, child development, and therapeutic recreation.

The No Child Left Behind Act of 2002 has created demand for specialists in assessment and remediation. Teachers are expected to use technology to enhance student learning. Educators also need to "mainstream," or integrate into the classroom, students with physical or mental disabilities and those who speak English as a second language. Schools are eager to hire minority teachers and male teachers.

In higher education, a large number of faculty members are approaching retirement. However, 30% of post-secondary instructors are part-time or temporary, a rate that may increase further, according to the American Association of University Professors. Graduates with Ph.D.'s who want to teach at the college level are most competitive if they have done cross-disciplinary work.

Demand for recipents of liberal arts doctorates varies year to year. Students earning doctoral degrees in educational or psychological measurement, cognitive science, special education, and learning disabilities are very marketable. Shortages are being reported for faculty to teach in medicine, nursing, and business.

In the sciences, it is becoming more common for employers to expect completion of two post-doctoral assignments. Over 80% of academic Ph.D. life scientists in the 1970s were tenured or in tenure-track positions, and less than 10% were in post-doctoral assignments. In 2000, about 50% of them were in positions with tenure potential and 18% were post-docs, revealed the National Academy of Sciences. The number of graduating biomedical Ph.D.'s is still far greater than jobs available to them as faculty members. The pharmaceutical and biotechnology industries are decreasing their hiring of researchers in drug discovery (basic research) in favor of drug development (regulatory approval, manufacturing, and marketing). A more favorable job market awaits graduates with doctoral degrees such as medicinal chemistry, and bioinformatics.

Entry-level opportunities for new graduates entering nonprofits include fundraising, event planning, community outreach, and volunteer recruitment. Other positions may include policy research and advocacy. Volunteers who have served the organization or a similar agency usually receive preference.

Healthcare

Health professions are attractive careers for students with an aptitude for science and an interest in helping people, with new hires in some fields receiving signing bonuses The Bureau of Labor Statistics forecasts that one in five new jobs, 4.7 million, will occur in healthcare by 2014. This industry includes almost 200 occupations, including the one with the most employees in the U.S.–nurse.

An aging U.S. population (77 million baby boomers) has high expectations of healthcare services. They remain active longer than did previous generations and are quick to use new technology. Increased demand can already be seen for cosmetic surgery, knee replacements, and treatment for cataracts. In addition, research has increased public awareness of health problems and treatments. More than 80 sleep disorders have been diagnosed, creating jobs for polysomnographic technologists and technicians. Contributing to public health research, cancer registrars track incidence types and outcomes of the disease. Eye and tissue bank specialists work with transplantation teams.

An expanding population has resulted in some Florida hospitals offering registered nurses signing bonuses of up to $15,000. According to the National Council of State Boards of Nursing, licensing exams will soon be offered in foreign countries due to an expected shortage of a million nurses. As a higher percentage of Americans are 60 years old and above, nurses will be needed in nursing care facilities and home health care settings. Nurses with graduate degrees in primary care--clinical nurse specialists, nurse practitioners, midwives, and anesthetists—will continue to find plentiful opportunities and salaries that can reach up to $170,000 a year. School nurses are also in short supply. An emerging area is forensic nursing, which involves obtaining evidence from victims of violence, who are often traumatized, and testifying in court.

In contrast to labor market projections in the 1990's of an oversupply of physicians, there are growing fears of a doctor shortage of crisis proportions. Physicians in primary care, medical research, reproductive endocrinology, geriatrics, and plastic surgery have been heavily recruited for some time. Demand has increased for physicians in cardiology, radiology, and surgery. An aging population is expected to increase the need for urologists, geriatricians, and ophthamologists. Medical school usually requires four years after the bachelor's degree. An additional one to seven years of further medical education is necessary in certain specialties.

Physical therapists must have a master's degree, and pharmacists require a Pharm.D. degree, which takes another one to two years of study after the bachelor's degree. Dentists and veterinarians attend four years of graduate training, with additional study required for specialization.

Demand is high for positions of rehabilitation counselors, speech-language pathologists, audiologists, orthoptists (eye muscle specialists), health care administrators, physician assistants, medical dosimetrists (radiation dosage specialists), all of which generally require post-graduate education.

Additional growth occupations in health fields that do not not require post-baccaulareate study include occupational therapists, orthotists and prosthetists (designers of devices for the disabled), dieticians, nuclear medicine technologists, dental hygienists, respiratory therapists, recreation therapists, and medical aestheticians (licensed skin care specialists).

Public health education may be entered by students with a related bachelor's degree, but a masters in public health makes applicants much more competitive. Some typical job titles include wellness program specialist, health educator, policy analyst, outreach specialist, and researcher. Insurance companies hire experienced professionals as disease management specialists, who identify members with chronic health conditions and encourage them to comply with treatment recommendations.

Government

Federal Government

The U.S. government is the largest employer in the world and expects to do high volume hiring in the next five years due to expected retirements of baby boomers.

Some occupations have a high concentration of jobs in the federal government, such as geographers (73%), mathematicians (46%), economists (32%), zoologists and wildlife biologists (32%), anthropologists and archeologists (27%), and physicists (26%).

The Department of Homeland Security has many job opportunities in areas of defense, intelligence, security, and emergency preparedness. According to the Education Department and Committee for Economic Development, the most critical foreign language skills for national security are Arabic, Chinese, Hindi, Japanese, Korean, Persian/Farsi, Russian, Turkish, and Urdu. Canada, Mexico, and China are the top trade partners with the United States, so Spanish and Chinese skills may be an asset for import/export specialists. Foreign language fluency in certain federal jobs earn employees annual bonuses of $5,000-$25,000.

Many federal government positions are open to students with any major or to those with a specific number of course hours in a subject. Geospatial intelligence positions, for example, are open to students in a variety of majors: astronomy, cartography, computer science, meteorology, environmental science, geography, geophysics, and international affairs. Job openings related to homeland security include investigative assistant, mission support assistant, and program assistant, among others. An advanced degree is required for a national security strategist position.

As a result of a serious backlog, the United States Patent and Trademark Office (USPTO) is offering a recruitment incentive of up to $9,900 annually to enhanced federal salary rates for electrical and computer engineers as patent examiners. Other majors eligible for hire as patent examiners include biology, chemistry, physics, chemical engineering, mechanical engineering, and computer science.

The federal government offers many programs for students during college and following graduation at several websites.

Part-time jobs, internships, co-ops, work-study jobs, and volunteer service: www.studentjobs.gov/

Jobs for college graduates: www.usajobs.gov

Today's Military: www.todaysmilitary.com

Making the difference (Hot Jobs; Cool Internships; Federal Student Loan Repayment Program; Red, White, and Blue Jobs: Making a Difference with Your Liberal Arts Degree): www.makingthedifference.org

State and Local Government

New positions are being added to state and local governments, such as coastal management specialist, junior urban designer, urban or environmental planner, entry level city planner, and conservation data technician. Applicants strengthen their candidacy with a master's degree, in disciplines such as coastal or natural resource management, landscape architecture, architecture, urban design, city planning, civil engineering, and urban/environmental planning, or with a master of public administration. Other positions available in government include photogrammetrists, who conduct aerial and space photography, and remote sensing specialists, who measure thermal and microwave energy.

Arts And Entertainment

According to the Bureau of Labor Statistics, 10 million new creative sector jobs are projected in the next decade. Arts, music, culture, and entertainment will add more than 400,000 jobs–twice as many as engineering. Richard Florida, author of *The Rise of the Creative Class*, predicts job growth where technology, consumer goods and entertainment intersect.

Computer game industry jobs include assistant community manager, a liaison between players and developers. A localization technician translates game components into a foreign language and ensures their compatibility with the new country's culture.

Marketing, Sales and Distribution

Global competition for consumer products is increasing the need for product or brand management employees. These marketing professionals oversee all aspects of promoting and distributing a particular brand, such as Ivory soap or Oreo cookies. Most brand managers have sales experience and an MBA. Some bachelor's degree recipients begin as a brand assistant, but most start as a sales representative.

In the last few years, positions have emerged such as bloggers and technical evangelists. Bloggers may coordinate online marketing activities, such as monitoring message boards, tracking success of promotional campaigns, distributing viral videos, and writing marketing content for an organization's website. Technical evanglists spread the word about new technological products. Some examples of entry-level jobs which are Internet-based are ad traffic coordinator and community producer, who conduct marketing activities for online newsletters and interactive community-based sites.

A population that is increasingly diverse has led to marketers who specialize in targeting racial and ethnic groups. Hispanics are the fastest growing minority group and are reached on Spanish-language television networks such as Univision and Telemundo. ImaginAsian offers media (films, DVD, theatre, radio, website) designed for consumers from Korean, Chinese, Japanese, and Indian backgrounds. Organizations often seek marketing specialists who are bilingual and bicultural.

Futurists help organizations anticipate the impact of demographic, technological, and regulatory trends on marketing, image, and hiring. They work at employers as varied as IBM, the FBI, and Hallmark.

Management trainees in retailing earn starting salaries in the mid-thirties to high forties, depending on store volume and location. Retailing is an entrepreneurial environment, with rapid advancement possible in expanding companies. Managers of "superstores" are responsible for volume of $12-100 million a year, supervising from 100-400 employees. With outstanding performance and willingness to relocate, these managers can earn $100,000+ within three to five years in this position. Retail opportunities also include loss prevention, operations management, and distribution, merchandising, and buying.

Science, Technology, Engineering, and Mathematics Careers

The U.S. government has spent billions of dollars on programs to address the inadequate number of college students and graduates entering science, technology, engineering, and mathematics fields. A General Accounting Office report in October 2005 indicates that "concerns have been raised about the nation's ability to maintain its global technological competitive advantage in the future." The number of college students graduating in the sciences has decreased each year since 1985 with one exception—biological sciences.

Biological and Physical Sciences

The Bureau of Labor Statistics predicts that jobs for life scientists will grow at triple the average rate for all occupations. Employers in biotechnology, bioagricultural, pharmaceutical, and clinical research organizations heavily recruit professionals required in drug discovery, manufacturing, and clinical trials. Some of these occupations include allied health professionals, pharmaceutical chemists, epidemiologists, regulatory affairs specialists, project managers, clinical research coordinators and analysts, biostatisticians, and SAS (statistical analysis) programmers. The diagnostic and medical devices industries are also hiring many scientists and engineers.

Biological/Life Science

Entry-level life science jobs in a lab setting include laboratory technician, quality lab associate, protein chemist, cytogenetic technician, trace evidence microscopist, forensic biology analyst, and antibody specialist. Science graduates who enjoy working with young people are sought by public schools to teach, whether or not they have a teaching certification.

A biology or chemistry major may work as a pharmaceutical or technical sales representative, customer assistance specialist, technical writer, clinical trial assistant or monitor (performing testing on new drugs). Life science majors may enter the field of environmental protection in positions such as research assistant, hazardous waste technician, and purification operator. A chemistry major may work as a creative fragrance associate in the perfume industry.

With an advanced degree in a life science, a graduate may qualify for jobs such as medicinal chemist, DNA development analyst, quality control analytical chemist, forensic scientist, serologist/DNA analyst, computational chemist, policy analyst, bioanalytical scientist, clinical trials researcher, and regulatory affairs manager.

Physical Science

The physical sciences are astronomy, earth sciences (geology, hydrology, meteorology, oceanography, soil science) and physics. A bachelor's degree qualifies a graduate for jobs such as assistant project geologist, hydrogeologist, air quality analyst/noise analyst, seismic data engineer, forensics specialist, electro-optics research analyst, satellite data analyst, process engineer, energy policy analyst, study analyst/technical writer, and middle school or secondary teacher. Physics majors are sought by Wall Street firms as quantitative analysts.

With an advanced degree, physical science graduates may be considered for jobs such as computational physicist, solid state physicist, climatologist, medical devices designer, seismologist, oceanographer, polymer physicist, and laser physicist. Nanotechnology is an emerging field with opportunities involving the structure of matter as small as atoms to create or improve products. Bionics, the use of new materials to replace or improve parts of the body, has led to development of cochlear implants, artificial hearts, and hands.

Agricultural/Environmental Science

Students in agricultural-related majors may qualify for jobs as an agronomy production specialist (crop protection), crop insurance agent, junior purchasing agent, and environmental (farm) compliance coordinator.

Jobs for environmental science majors include environmental health and safety technologist, conservation data technician, air/noise quality analyst, environmental monitor, land conservation specialist, recycling coordinator/specialist, wastewater laboratory technician, environmental assessor, and fire ecology specialist.

With an advanced degree, graduates may qualify for a job as a research forester, program associate in forest stewardship, ecological researcher, recycling project manager, and water/wastewater engineer. Potential risk management positions for these scientists are environmental research associate, occupational risk assessment researcher, environmental impact analyst, environmental planner/field monitor, natural resource specialist (air monitoring quality assurance), environmental resource analyst, policy analyst, or GIS (geographic information system) scientist.

Computer and Information Science

Contrary to popular belief, not all of the jobs in information technology and computer science are going to India and China. In fact, there is a strong demand for new graduates with degrees and skills in these areas. Renny DiPentima, chief executive of SRA International, described the 2005 job market in computer science to *U.S. News & World Report*:

....

"It's like running out of iron ore in the middle of the industrial revolution. We are in an information-technology revolution, and in certain areas we are running out of knowledge workers."

....

Marjorie Bynum of the Information Techology Association of America gives this advice: "Job prospects appear best for people with technical skills and business abilities. Employers want people who understand the intersection of business and the application of IT." Executives also value computer scientists who have experience interacting with engineering staff and customers.

Computer science is also intersecting with the arts in the entertainment industry to expand its products and services. The new frontier of marketing is digital and interactive media–advertising on cell phones, computer games, TV-on-demand, e-mail, and the Internet. Traditional advertising is increasingly at a disadvantage when compared to integrated communications. Web designers skilled in computer graphics, visual design, marketing, and ecommerce play an important role in Internet marketing.

The growth rate for video-games is projected to be 16.5%, more than television (7%), or music (2%), according to market research company IDC. The mobile gaming industry is expected to more than double from 2005-2008 ($600 million to $1500 million), employing many computer scientists.

Web analytics is the process of using technology to measure effectiveness of Internet marketing, such as attracting visitors to an organization's website, registering potential buyers, or increasing purchases of users. The goal of an Internet marketing firm is to improve an organization's return on investment through optimizing its web site results.

A new graduate may test keywords and copy provided to search engines and directories, encouraging users to click on an ad. Sample job titles in website marketing are search engine optimization (SEO) analyst, pay-per-click specialist, landing page optimization analyst, web analytics specialist, and web audience analyst. The SEO field is expected to generate $11.6 billion in business by 2010, nearly tripling volume from 2004. Employers typically prefer majors such as MIS, computer science, mathematics, computational linguistics, and statistics for Internet marketing jobs.

A large number of new computer or information science jobs will be interdisciplinary, such as the following:

INTERDISCIPLINARY JOBS REQUIRING TECHNICAL SKILLS

Occupations	Skills
Data miner, search engine analyst, marketing researcher, blogger, competitive intelligence analyst	Marketing, web analytics, statistics, information science, usability design
Bioinformatics, computational biologist	Software engineering, biology, statistics
Usability specialist	Usability research, web design, psychology, technical writing
Instructional designer, technology infusion specialist	Educational technology, distance learning, web design
Animation specialist, graphic designer, game designer	Art (drawing), graphic design, computer graphics, computer programming, creative writing
GIS analyst, data specialist, mapping specialist	IT (GIS software), statistics, geography, city planning, cartography, geology

Information architect	Information science, human factors, usability design

Engineering

Even though almost 70,000 engineers graduated last year in the United States, it was not enough to satisfy employer demand. Congress passed a $286.5 billion bill to repair and construct highways, which is expected to increase openings for civil engineers by 17% until 2014. Environmental engineers will benefit from the need to replace or upgrade sewer and water-treatment facilities, with number of jobs projected to be 27% higher by 2017. The openings most in demand in 2006 are "hybrids of management and technology," according to the National Center on Education and the Economy. Strong demand exists for technical skills, which can be enhanced with with industry-specific knowledge, interpersonal, teamwork, and business skills.

The job market is good for engineers with specialization in petroleum, electrical, computer, software, chemical, materials, and mechanical. Other fields where engineers are needed include testing, product engineering, analog/mixed signal design, and global positioning systems.

Environmental scientists have backgrounds in engineering, chemistry, or environmental science. They are employed by the government as environmental health inspectors and by industry as industrial hygienists and environmental managers to help organizations comply with government regulations regarding hazardous waste, pollutants, recycling and other responsibilities. Emerging technologies are expected to create many related jobs. The three technologies most often cited for projected job growth are biotechnology, nanotechnology, optics and photonics.

Mathematics

"There has never been a better time to be a mathematician," according to a National Security Agency executive quoted in the January 23, 2006 Business Week article, "Math will Rock Your World." The Society for Industrial and Applied Mathematics (SIAM) predicts that emerging occupations requiring mathematics expertise will include computational biology and genomics, data mining, neuroscience, material science, computer animation and data imaging. In cryptology, mathematics is used to protect communications which must be secure.

Risk and decision science has become an expanding field, with openings for entry-level and advanced degree graduates. In addition to degrees in risk and decision or management science, other qualifying majors may include economics, finance, accounting, business administration, engineering, computer science, and mathematics. Typical job titles include risk assessor, decision science analyst, management science analyst, operations research analyst, and quality control analyst. Risk and decision science professionals use analytical skills such as computer modeling, process improvement, and other quantitative methods to solve problems.

Applied mathematics includes jobs in statistics, actuarial science, operations research, and financial engineering. The biotechnology and pharmaceutical industries are major industries that recruit students with degrees in biostatistics. The *Jobs Rated Almanac* has listed actuary as one of the top four most desirable occupations due to compensation, challenge, job security, and work-life balance. Operations research uses advanced analytical methods (i.e. simulation, optimization, and probability) to assist with complex decision-making. Financial engineering is a field in which mathematical models are used to create new financial products in banking, investment and risk management. "Quants" can enter the lucrative fields of private equity and hedge funds.

Social, Behavioral and Economic Sciences

The American Psychological Association (APA) has labeled the period of 2000-2010 as the "Decade of Behavior," highlighting social problems which behavioral scientists could help prevent.

Social science graduates work for government agencies, policy institutes, nonprofits, consulting firms, and "think tanks" to research and report on the results of programming related to social, educational, and public health projects. These organizations study social problems such as crime, poverty, drug abuse, and high school dropout rate.

Professional Services

Consulting and Investment Banking

Fast Company magazine describes consulting and investment banking as "extreme jobs." Consulting and investment banking are high in mystique and glamour on college campuses. These industries attract many of the best students, with some employers requiring applicants to have a GPA of at least 3.5--or even 3.8--to qualify. Many parents are surprised to learn that the fields of consulting and investment banking are open to new bachelor's degree graduates.

Consulting firms seek students who have excelled academically. Some prefer course work such as computer science, engineering, other sciences, and business. New hires usually begin as staff consultants or business analysts. Consulting usually involves frequent travel and heavy overtime. An MBA is typically needed for advancement in management consulting (as opposed to systems consulting). Consulting firms frequently specialize in fields such as information systems, benefits and compensation, health care, and environmental work and may also recruit for related advanced degree.

Investment banks value diversity in applicants' backgrounds, but also demand high GPAs and math aptitude, as evidenced by SAT scores and college transcripts. New graduates typically begin as financial analysts. Training programs provide the specific skills new hires need for number-crunching and analytic work. An 80-hour work week is common in investment banking.

The duration of most financial analyst programs is two years. It is increasingly common for exceptional analysts to be promoted to associates without an MBA. An MBA is necessary to advance to associate and higher-level positions in some firms. Financial analysts may earn salaries of $55,000-60,000 a year, with year-end bonuses that may double their income to six figures. (Also see Chapters 6 and 7.)

Competition is keen for both consulting and investment banking jobs, and the work is very demanding. Both fields provide intellectual challenge, task variety, and lucrative compensation.

Accounting and Finance

High demand exists for accountants, auditors, management consultants, and investment bankers. Sarbanes-Oxley regulations, which standardize corporate disclosure of financial status and institute safeguards against fraud, have created a need for accountants to implement or audit the new procedures.

Although accounting graduates are in high demand, student enrollment in this field has dropped by 20%, according to the American Institute of Certified Public Accountants. Accounting firms are recruiting sophomore and junior accounting students for internships and part-time jobs to develop a pool of job applicants with applied experience. To become an accountant qualified to sit for the CPA exam requires 150 semester hours of course work, which usually takes one year beyond a four-year bachelor's degree program. Bachelor's degree recipients may earn a master's of accounting in one year at many universities.

Bachelors-level recipients are hired for financial management trainee positions in corporations, performing a mix of accounting, pricing, forecasting, and budgeting duties. They are also recruited as loan officers for banks, credit unions, mortgage companies, and automobile dealers. Commercial banks, whose customers are individuals and small businesses, have entry-level openings for personal bankers, credit analysts, and management trainees, among other jobs.

Some consulting firms have openings for financial analysts to work on client engagements. Investment banks--whose customers include large corporations, pension funds, and government entities, among others--hire analysts to research background material for potential mergers and acquisitions, initial stock offerings, and portfolio investments. New graduates may also work as traders. Many employers prefer to hire students with quantitative majors for financial analyst positions, while others will consider any major who has earned good grades in one or two accounting courses.

Insurance companies recruit for sales positions and entry-level jobs in underwriting, claims, loss control, and other fields.

Law

Law is a popular career interest for students, but law school admission is very competitive and the job market for lawyers is tight. Large law school enrollments will result in a continuing difficult job market for those who attend less prestigious institutions. Law schools award a J.D. degree after a three-year course of study beyond the bachelor's degree.

Two legal specialties in high demand are corporate law and intellectual property law. Sarbanes-Oxley regulations have created strong demand for lawyers with a specialty in securities and corporate governance. Emerging technologies have made intellectual property law important, especially for lawyers with a science background. (The importance of protecting intangible capital is also likely to create jobs for scientists, advertisers, web designers, and salespersons.) An aging population may also increase the need for estate planning lawyers.

Paralegal and legal research positions are in high demand. Some law firms and government agencies hire graduates with any major and provide on-the-job training for these positions. For example, one law firm considers applicants with a four-year degree, a minimum 3.0 GPA, and who are willing to make a two-year commitment.

Other employers prefer applicants who have completed paralegal training, which may be obtained through certificate programs in a few months or through degree programs lasting two to four years. Advancement opportunities for paralegals include positions as a legal assistant manager and litigation support manager, with average compensation of $97,000 a year or more.

Undergraduate Fellowships

Research fellowships have traditionally been available to students completing graduate degree programs, but some are now designed for new bachelor's degree recipients. A student may want to obtain more research experience to increase his or her competitiveness for medical or graduate school. Perhaps a new graduate needs time to save money for graduate school or to confirm a career direction. Undergraduate fellowships are very selective and offered by government agencies, corporations, and universities such as the following:

Government agencies: www.science.gov/internships/undergrad.html

EPA: es.epa.gov/ncer/fellow/

Department of Homeland Security: www.orau.gov/dhsed/

Council on Undergraduate Research: www.cur.org/UGSF.html

Summer Undergraduate Research Fellowship:
www.surf.nist.gov/surf2.htm

International

Many students are interested in international business, but not many employers, other than some consulting firms, hire a new graduate for an overseas business assignment. The U.S. Department of State hires new graduates as foreign service specialists. The United Nations has a limited number of openings abroad for junior professionals. Some businesses have entry-level positions for import/export specialists. Maersk, an international shipping company, has global opportunities through its entry level programs.

Work experience, language skills, and travel abroad may eventually lead to work in a foreign country. The biggest competitors for the U.S. are expected to be China and India, so area studies of those countries may be helpful. Some companies prefer an MBA for overseas employment.

The Family Business

According to *Family Business Review*, at least 80 percent of businesses in the U.S. are family owned, employing 62 percent of the nation's workforce. About 30 percent of family businesses continue through its second generation, 12 percent last into the third generation, and 3 percent persist into at least the fourth-generation.

Some students procrastinate in their job search, rationalizing that they can always join the family business, whether or not they are sincerely interested in it. In contrast, other students may feel obligated—or even pressured—to join the family firm.

If a family member owns a business, you may want to discuss its employment needs and your child's assumptions about how it fits into his or her plans. Students may be inspired by exposure to entrepreneurship and want to start their own business. Over 1,500 colleges offer majors, minors, courses, or special programs in entrepreneurship, according to the Kauffman Foundation.

* * *

Answers to Quiz on Page 29

1. d	6. b
2. d	7. d
3. d	8. c
4. c	9. b
5. b	10. d

Table 2.1

ACCOUNTING, BANKING AND FINANCE

Field	Job Titles	Average Compen-sation	Job Growth	Typical Major(s)
Accounting Private/Corp Public	Staff accountant	 $47,975 $46,289	 Faster than Average	 Accounting, Business
Auditing Private/Corp Public	Auditor	 $50,435 $48,598	 Faster than Average	 Accounting, Business
Commercial Banking	Personal banker Lending officer	$36,297 $39,688	Slower than Average	Any major (preferably with 1-2 accounting courses)
Investment Banking	Financial analyst Assistant trader	$49,776 $55,063 +bonus	Slower than Average (market fluctuations)	Business, Economics, or any major with high math aptitude and computer skills
Finance/ Economics	Management trainee Corporate finance Assistant economist Loan assistant	$31,988	Slower than Average	Business, Economics

Table 2.2

MARKETING AND RELATED FIELDS

Field	Job Titles	Average Compensation	Job Growth	Typical Major(s)
Advertising	Production assistant, assistant copywriter, media assistant	$38,136	Faster than Average	Advertising, English Journalism, Psychology, any major
Brand/Product Management	Brand assistant	$47,536	Faster than Average	Business, any major
Buying/ Merchandising	Department management trainee, assistant buyer	$41,531	Slower than Average	Business, Liberal Arts any major
Customer Service	Customer service representative, technical support agent	$32,305	Faster than Average	Sciences, Computer science, any major
Marketing Research	Associate analyst	$43,489	Faster than Average	Math/Statistics, Business, Economics
Sales	Sales representative, marketing representative	$39,316	Faster than Average	Any major, Business

Table 2.3

OTHER BUSINESS FIELDS

Field	Job Titles	Average Compensation	Job Growth	Typical Major(s)
Consulting	Staff consultant Business analyst	$51,120 + bonus potential	Much Faster than Average	Computer Science, Applied Math, Business, any major
Hospitality	Hotel management trainee; food service/ restaurant/ management trainee	$37,211	Average	Hotel or Restaurant Management, any major
Human Resources	Staffing specialist, compensation analyst, employee relations trainee	$39,007	Faster than Average	Business, Human Resources, Psychology, any major
Customer Service	Customer service representative, technical support agent	$32,305	Faster than Average	Sciences, Computer Science, any major
Marketing Research	Junior/associate analyst, coder/editor, telephone interviewer	$43,489	Faster than Average	Math/Statistics ,Business, Economics, Psychology

Table 2.4

MATH AND COMPUTER SCIENCE

Field	Job Titles	Average Compen- sation	Job Growth	Typical Major(s)
Math/ Statistics	Mathematician, statistician research assistant	$46,401	Slower than Average	Applied Math, Statistics, Mathematics Computer Science
Actuarial Science	Actuarial assistant	$56,821	Faster than Average	Actuarial Science, Mathematics Statistics, Business, Finance
Computer Science	Computer programmer	$46,211	More slowly than Average	Computer Science, Math - related
	Systems analyst/designer	$51,011	Much faster than Average	
	Technical support technician	$41,122	Faster than Average	
Info.Science /Systems	Computer specialist, database administrator, user interface designer	$49.992	Faster than Average	Information Science, Computer Science, any major with specified skills

Table 2.5

ENGINEERING AND CONSTRUCTION

Field	Job Titles	Average Compensation	Job Growth	Typical Major(s)
Engineering	Aerospace engineer	$52,131	Slower	Aerospace Engineering
	Biomedical engineer	$55,283	Much Faster	Biomedical Engineering
	Chemical engineer	$59,707	Average	Chemical Engineering
	Civil engineer	$47,750	Average	Civil Engineering
	Electrical/electronics engineer	$54,915	Average	Electrical or Electronics Engineering
	Environmental engineer	$54,945	Much Faster	Environmental Engineering
	Hardware design/development	$56,463	Average	Computer Engineering
	Manufacturing/ Industrial	$54,911	Average	Industrial Engineering
	Materials engineer	$55,230	Average	Materials Engineering
	Mechanical engineer	$54,695	Average	Mechanical Engineering
	Systems engineer	$55,309	Much Faster	Computer Engineering
Construction	Assistant project manager, estimator	$46,506	Average	Construction or Civil Engineering

Table 2.6

LIFE AND PHYSICAL SCIENCES

Field	Job Titles	Average Compensation	Job Growth	Typical Major(s)
Agricultural Business	Commodity merchant, logistics specialist, production supervisor	$38,055	Average	Agriculture, Agribusiness Economics
Biological Science/Life Science	Research assistant, Lab technician	$36,962	Average	Biology or related
Chemistry	Research technician, quality control chemist	$43,465	Slower than Average	Chemistry or related
Construction Management	Estimator, purchasing agent, sales counselor, draftsperson, land manager	$46,506	Average	Any major, depending on position
Geoscience	Geologist	$40,430	Slower than Average	Geology, Earth Science, Environmental Studies

Table 2.7

COMMUNICATIONS

Field	Job Titles	Average Compensation	Job Growth	Typical Major(s)
Journalism	Reporter, news analyst	$36,900	Average	Journalism, English, any major
Public Relations	Public relations specialist	$34,143	Average	Public Relations, Journalism, any major
Communications	Technical writer, Editorial assistant	$33,418	Average	English, Journalism, Science Major, any major
Production	Production assistant, camera operator, announcer	$30,300	Average	Broadcast Journalism, any major

Table 2.8

GOVERNMENT

Field	Job Titles	Average Compen-sation	Job Growth	Typical Major(s)
Executive and Legislative	Legislative assistant, Research assistant	$25,623* or $31,740	Average	Any major, Political Science
Law Enforcement	Police officer, special agent	$41,000	Average	Any major, Sociology/ Criminology
Regulation	Inspector, compliance officer	$25,623* or $31,740	Depends on position	Depends on position, technical or any major
Homeland Security	Investigative assistant, mission support assistant, program assistant	$25,623* or $31,740	Faster than Average, depends on position	Technical major, any major
Military	Second lieutenant, Ensign	$48,114 (with allowances)	Faster than Average	Depends on specialty
Social Services	Restitution specialist, victim or witness advocate, protective services coordinator, re-settlement coordinator	$25,623* or $31,740	Faster than Average	Social Science, any major

*Salaries may depend on education, position, location, and security clearance.

Summary

....

Factors to consider in career choice:

- Job duties

- Advancement opportunities

- Compensation and benefits

- Job market demand

- Societal trends, such as the aging of the population, legislation, and political events, such as 9/11

- Aptitude and motivation

- Working conditions, including work/life balance

- Potential to join a family business

Hot Career Fields

- Can be difficult to predict and subject to rapid change.

- Are likely to be found in these fields:

  *Professional business services

  *Health professions and life sciences

  *Math-related, computer science, and information science

  *Materials science

  *Marketing

  *Emergency management and business continuity; homeland security

Entry-Level Jobs for Bachelor's Graduates:

- Available to any major in a wide variety of fields
- Available to specific majors in more technical fields

Conversation Starters for Parents and Students

1. What do you consider your biggest accomplishment? Which of your activities do you enjoy the most? What achievement or activity has made you feel most proud of your efforts?

2. What is your favorite course? Is it also the course where you earned the best grades? If not, why not?

3. How would you describe the ideal job for you?

4. What are some of the advantages of career choices you have considered? What are some of the risks or disadvantages?

5. How would some of your career options affect other aspects of your life, such as family, hobbies, volunteer work, etc.?

6. (If relevant) What are your thoughts about joining the family business?

Resources

America's Career Info Net: www.onestopcoach.org

Career Overview: www.careeroverview.com

Career Voyages (section for parents, videos): careervoyages.gov/

U.S. Department of Labor: www.bls.gov/emp/home.htm

Occupational Outlook Handbook (Bureau of Labor Statistics):
www.bls.gov/oco/

The Princeton Review Online: www.princetonreview.com/cte/default.asp

Sloan Career Cornerstone Center(section for parents on careers in science, technology, engineering, mathematics, and computing career planning: www.careercornerstone.org/

Hot Jobs for the Future: www.careerplanner.com/Career-Articles/Hot_jobs.htm

My Cool Career: www.mycoolcareer.com (section for parents)

What Color is Your Parachute?
Richard Bolles, Ten Speed Press (updated yearly)

The Student's Federal Career Guide
Kathryn Kraemer Troutman and Emily K. Troutman, The Résumé Place
(2004), www.tenstepsforstudents.org/pages/test.html

CHAPTER 3

CHOOSING A MAJOR: DRAMA VS. ACCOUNTING

Don't despair if your child is having difficulty choosing, or staying with, a major. More than half of college freshmen are undecided about their major, and it is estimated that half to two thirds of all college students change their major at least once. Some students change their major so frequently they could qualify for the "Major of the Month Club"!

Eventually, though, and at most schools by the end of the sophomore year, your son or daughter will have to select a major, even if only temporarily. And sooner or later, if he or she is to graduate, at least one major will have to be settled upon. How should it be done?

Like choosing a career, there is unfortunately no magic formula or test to give the answer. But there are some important considerations. The self-assessment and career research discussed in Chapter 1 will help narrow down possible career options. The career choice, if known early enough, may define the major. Architecture, engineering, education, and many of the health and allied health fields (such as clinical laboratory science/medical technology, pharmacy, and physical therapy), are examples of fields in which the career and major are identical. Even these fields, though, can be entered later through other routes (such as programs of study as short as one year after a bachelor's degree), so it is not essential that a student major in them in order to ever work in them.

A known career choice may also suggest *several* possible majors, giving the student the option to choose the one that is most appealing. For example, the student interested in a sales career might major in business, psychology, or communications.

Students may initially select a major based on a hobby or interest and may consider making a career of this interest. They may find, though, that studying a subject is different from having an avocational interest in it. The student who enjoys tinkering with cars, stargazing, or working with animals may discover that the rigorous disciplines of mechanical engineering, astronomy, or zoology are not what he wants to study for four or more years.

What if your child is undecided upon a career or is thinking of careers in radically different disciplines: music versus business. Keeping in mind that he or she probably has about two years before having to declare a major, encourage your child to take several courses in areas of interest. An introductory course in anthropology or accounting may spark a desire to pursue these subjects further, or a few courses in music may help your child realize that majoring in math would be preferable.

A student who is still having trouble choosing between two majors of interest after having taken a few courses in both might want to base the decision on the employment demand for the majors, information that can be obtained from the career office. Although students with the proper preparation can find satisfactory work regardless of their major, students in some majors are likely to have less difficulty than others.

Cary, a sophomore, was interested in both philosophy and business. After research and discussion with his career and academic advisors, he decided to major in business, the more "marketable" degree, but to continue to take philosophy courses as his schedule would allow.

Another student, Emily, enjoyed her courses in biology and journalism. She chose journalism as her major and supplemented it with biology and other science coursework in order to prepare for a career as a science writer.

Students should major in something they enjoy. Not only are they more likely to stick with it, but they will also make better grades, have greater interest, and not look at the academic side of college merely as something they must endure as a means to an end - a diploma. Of course, students may basically enjoy the major they have chosen yet still encounter a particular course, professor, or required elective that they intensely dislike. Sometimes they *do* have to endure it as a means to an end! For example, students majoring in the sciences, health disciplines, or computer science may be required to take organic chemistry, physics, or calculus. These courses can be quite difficult for many students and can scare students out of the major. Also, some students avoid math and science courses because faculty in these disciplines usually have a reputation for grading more stringently.

If the problem is only with one or two courses and the student can get through them, possibly with tutoring, he or she should not be scared off. On the other hand, a change of major should be considered if the major will require many courses in subjects that he or she finds extremely hard or uninteresting. (Sometimes the decision to change is essentially made for students because they are unable to pass the course needed to advance to the next level.)

Which Comes First—The Major Or The Career Choice?

Is it better to choose a major based on one's career interest or to choose a career based on one's major? This is a chicken-or-egg question. Some students could not possibly base a decision about their major on their career interests because their interests are still very vague. These students typically choose a general liberal arts major, like psychology, biology, or political science. Those who have fairly well defined career interests are likely to select a major that relates at least minimally to those interests: the student interested in advertising may choose to major in English or journalism; the student interested in computer programming may major in mathematics or computer science; or the student interested in social services may major in psychology or sociology.

Students may incorrectly assume that a particular major is required or desirable for their career goal. For example, students interested in careers in investment banking sometimes think that they must major in business. Actually, investment banks recruiting bachelor's level candidates consider students of all majors. Their requirements typically include exceptionally high grades and test scores (such as SAT, GRE, LSAT, or GMAT), as well as leadership and internship experiences. According to a recruiter from a major New York investment bank, " To me, the key is that when we hire at the undergraduate level we're not looking for candidates to have existing knowledge; rather, we're looking for aptitude (in the form of test scores and much else besides) and interest in the work we do."

Often students aspiring to law school believe that political science or history is the right major to choose. In reality, there are no *required* majors for admission. Here is how one prestigious law school responds to the question of the best major: "As to a course of study while in college, there is no right answer to this question ….Every year we admit applicants who majored in virtually any conceivable discipline. That said, the law deals with every facet of human activity, and a lawyer should be a person with a broad base of knowledge and a range of intellectual interests. A reasonable degree of exposure to such subjects as history, literature, English composition, philosophy, political science, and economics will provide a good background for a full appreciation of the law. Whatever the courses selected, one should look for classes that require reading complex primary source material, analyzing it closely, and presenting well-reasoned conclusions in writing. One can find that preparation in almost any of the rigorous academic disciplines in a college or university."

Students planning to apply to MBA programs often mistakenly think that an undergraduate major in business is required, but MBA schools are open to all majors. Karen Ball, Assistant Director of Admissions at the University of Virginia's Darden School of Business, states:

....

"It is a common misperception that MBA programs want only business majors, when in fact we select from many majors. MBA programs want well-rounded, academically sound, future leaders, and the undergraduate major is less important in the admissions process. We attempt to compile a class of many different majors/backgrounds, which includes anything from Engineering to English to Business. Practically speaking, when we have prospective students coming from liberal arts backgrounds, we usually suggest that they take an accounting and/or statistics course to familiarize themselves with the material prior to coming to our program."

....

An increasing number of MBA schools, such as the University of Pennsylvania's Wharton School of Business, have accelerated programs ("3-2" programs) for students with undergraduate business majors. The University of Rochester describes its 3-2 program this way:

"In this program, students earn both a bachelor's degree in an undergraduate major and a master of business administration degree in five years. In three years of undergraduate study, students complete their majors and distribution requirements. Between January and March of their junior year, qualified students apply to the SimonSchool. The first year of the M.B.A. program is substituted for the senior year."

Some MBA programs offer a Pre-Term Program, a four-week summer session to ensure that all incoming MBA students have sufficient knowledge of financial accounting, microeconomics, and statistics. Optional classes are also offered on personal computer skills, which are necessary for coursework. First-year MBA students may also be tested on their knowledge of mathematics, including college-level calculus, which they must pass before beginning classes.

Medical schools no longer require a science or pre-med major, although they do require several specific science courses. According to one university's pre-med adviser:

> *"They all require at least the following: 2 semesters of Biology; 2 semesters of Inorganic Chemistry; 2 semesters of Organic Chemistry; and 2 semesters of Physics. All of these courses should be taken with the accompanying laboratory. Some schools have additional requirements such as a year of calculus or a course in biochemistry."*

However, one liberal arts major commented to his college career advisor that taking more science courses than recommended would have probably helped him score higher on the Medical College Admissions Test (MCAT).

Students should check with the career office, employers, graduate or professional school admissions officers, people working in fields of interest, as well as other students and faculty in the prospective major before making a final decision about their major.

Selecting A Major That Isn't Career-Related

Parents may worry if their child wishes to choose a major that doesn't readily point to a career or is in a field that seems impractical or impossibly competitive. Their children pick up on these fears. "You would just *die* if I became a theater major, wouldn't you?" Stacey, a junior in high school, asked her mother. The truth is, her mother (one of the authors) didn't die:

Stacey graduated from college as a theater major and is now successfully working in musical theater, with her mother being one of her proudest supporters.

Career counselors often see students who want to major in a field like art or music, but whose parents want them to major in business or some other applied major. Some parents even threaten to withdraw financial support if their child doesn't major in something that the parents consider practical.

It is natural to worry about whether our children will be able to find a job once they graduate. (If there weren't a need to be concerned, this book wouldn't be necessary.) But the major itself is rarely the cause of a graduate's difficulty finding employment. It is true that a few majors, like special education, pharmacy, or accounting, are very much in demand (as of this writing), so graduates of these majors generally find jobs easily; however, most students who plan well and have decent grades can find work regardless of their major.

There is a direct relationship between the college major and job upon graduation for only slightly more than 50% of college graduates. (The number is higher for certain fields, like education, engineering, and nursing.) Later in a graduate's career, the job is even less likely to be related to the graduate's major. So although the communications or philosophy major may not necessarily be employed in his or her field, the major itself is not a one-way ticket to unemployment or underemployment.

Many campus recruiters will interview any major. This does not mean, though, that recruiters will interview any candidate: they are quite particular about whom they will see. Although the request may not specify a particular major, it often does specify a certain GPA, work experience (part-time work or internship), and coursework such as six hours of accounting. The career plan and enhancers discussed in Chapter 1 can make a great difference in a senior's being able to obtain campus interviews and in the success of those interviews.

When An Early Choice Of Major Is Optimal

During the first two years your son or daughter will probably be taking primarily liberal arts or general education courses unless he or she has decided upon a major that requires early pre-requisites or courses that must be taken in sequence. A freshman or sophomore who has already decided to major in a field such as business, accounting, engineering, architecture, science, mathematics, computer science, or health sciences should enroll as early as possible in the courses required for the major: often these majors require many prerequisites, which must be taken in sequence. Some of these courses may only be offered one semester a year. Your son or daughter's academic adviser will help him or her select the courses required.

Students who have not yet made a definite decision but are considering majoring in engineering, mathematics, science, or health sciences should take the more difficult math courses (e.g. calculus) and organic chemistry (for those with interests in science or health) as freshmen or sophomores; otherwise, they may find their options to major in these subjects limited or they may have to backtrack in order to obtain the necessary prerequisites.

Some students change their major so often that they have far more credits than they need to graduate by their senior year, yet do not have the required courses in the major they have finally settled on. They may need to stay as much as one or two additional years in order to obtain the "right" credits.

Getting Accepted Into
The Desired Major

A few colleges or universities accept students directly into their desired major or "school" during the admissions process. Students attending these institutions, therefore, are assured as freshmen that they may enroll in the School of Business or School of Design or School of Education, etc. Most colleges and universities, though, do not require students to declare a major before their sophomore year. This is an advantage because it allows students to explore various subject areas without feeling pressure to make an early decision; yet it can be a problem for students without high grades who want to major in a discipline that has limited enrollment. Many colleges have a limited number of spaces in majors such as architecture, engineering, business, accounting, and the health areas (like pharmacy, nursing, and physical therapy). Students must generally apply as sophomores for admission to these programs. Admission usually requires a minimum GPA of 2.7 or 3.0 or higher (on a 4.0 scale) as well as an application that may ask for an essay and information about summer and part-time work experience or extracurricular activities. Students considering majors with limited enrollment should seek information as early as possible, preferably as freshmen, in order to know what they will need to be competitive for admission.

What if your son or daughter is denied admission to the major he or she wants? Our first recommendation is to talk to the dean or administrator of the program; ask why admission was denied and discuss the possibility of reapplying. Sometimes a student can improve grades or acquire sufficient work experience (through volunteer or part-time work) in order to be admitted in a semester or so. It is important for the student to assess, with advice from the program administrator, how likely it is that he or she will be admitted within a reasonable period of time. Some students stay on and on at a college, continuing to hope that they will gain admission to the School of Design, for example, and never do. In the meantime, they may have spent six or more years of time (and *their parents' money*) instead of being realistic and moving on with an alternative plan.

One alternative might be to select another major that is close to the desired one and will allow the student to enter his or her chosen career field. An example of this is to major in economics if admission to the business major is denied. Another option is to choose a less-competitive major in a similar career field, such as choosing occupational therapy rather than the highly competitive physical therapy. A third option is to take coursework or to "minor" in the desired area. Students denied admission to an accounting program, for example, will find that six to nine hours of accounting coursework is sufficient for many employment opportunities in banking and finance. A last alternative is to transfer to an institution where admission to the desired program is less competitive. Counselors from the university counseling center and career office can help students explore their options.

The Importance Of Grades

When selecting a major, students should consider how well they are likely to do in it and how important grades are for their intended career. In a recent study of 100 employers who hire new college graduates, 55% have specific GPA requirements, generally a 3.0, but in some cases as high as 3.5 or even 3.9. If your child is struggling in a major and is barely able to maintain a 2.5 GPA, he or she might consider changing to a less difficult major.

It can be particularly difficult for students with low GPA's in majors like mathematics, computer science, chemistry, physics, accounting, and engineering to find employment in fields related to their major, especially when the job market is competitive. Certain career fields like consulting and investment banking are open to any major but require very high grades (typically over a 3.4). Students considering graduate or professional school, for which a high GPA is usually important, should select a major that will both meet the course requirements for the graduate program in which they are interested and will be one in which they can excel.

Your son or daughter may have a strong interest in a subject and wish to major in it in spite of the fact that he or she isn't making high grades. Not all fields or employers emphasize grades. Fields like sales, retail, hospitality, human resources, and the arts, as well as smaller employers, tend to value experience and demonstrated interest over grades. Nevertheless, it is important to check in advance to know the consequences of low grades. Your son or daughter can obtain this information by talking with potential employers, people working in fields of interest, and the career office.

How Useful Are Minors?

Most students take only about one-third to one-half of their coursework in their major. They may be required to take many other courses in order to meet requirements of the general university or of the particular school that houses their major. For instance, often the School of Humanities or Liberal Arts requires two years of a foreign language, whereas the School of Engineering or Business may not. Some universities also require, or at least allow, a minor. Minors can enhance a student's credentials if they are selected wisely. For example, a student wanting a career in international affairs might major in political science and minor in a language like Spanish or Russian. Minors can also be an alternate route to a major that may not be offered: A student interested in management information systems attending a college that does not offer this major may simulate it by majoring in computer science and minoring in business, or vice-versa.

Students may be required or permitted to select a concentration, special option, or track within their major. Examples are a business administration major with a concentration in finance or mathematical sciences major in the statistics track. Concentrations, tracks, and options allow students to develop strength and specialization in an area of interest.

The Interdisciplinary Major

Some colleges offer the option of an "interdisciplinary major," which can serve the same purpose as a major-minor combination. Usually the interdisciplinary major consists of course work from three subject areas combined in a planful way; this major must be approved by the student's academic advisor. Kira, a student at a large university without a major in hospitality, was interested in convention management. She received approval for an interdisciplinary major in business, psychology, and recreation administration. In addition to her major, she prepared a career plan that included volunteer work and internships at a hotel owned by her university and at the university's activities center, which sponsored many concerts and large events. Upon graduation, she was hired as an assistant to a city convention manager.

What About Double Majors?

How useful are double majors? Students often assume that if one major is good, two are twice as good. In a recent survey of 125 employers, only 7% indicate that a double major is definitely more valuable than one major for gaining an entry-level position. Like minors, double (or even triple!) majors can be helpful if the student has a particular career goal in mind. A double major in health policy and business, for example, is ideal for the student interested in hospital administration. Similarly, a double major in advertising and economics is desirable for a student wanting to enter the non-creative side of advertising, such as being an account executive.

However, a double major in psychology and sociology or in history and political science rarely enhances a student's qualifications in the eyes of employers. Of course a student may wish to double-major or take an optional minor for the intellectual stimulation or simply to study a second area in depth.

Often students have to work tremendously hard to meet all of the requirements for two majors. They may have many labs or special projects like art shows or music performances that can be very time consuming.

Striving to meet the demands of two majors may cause a student to have lower grades, participate in fewer extracurricular activities, and feel a great deal of stress. It can delay a student's graduation by as much as a year (See Chapter 4, How Long Should It Take?) or prevent a student from participating in a valuable academic experience such as study abroad or a service-learning course. In a survey of one hundred campus recruiters, only six thought that a double major was definitely valuable for gaining an entry-level position with their organization. Students should carefully consider the costs versus the payoff of a double major.

B.A. versus B.S.

In some fields, like math or chemistry, students must choose between the bachelor of arts (B.A.) and the bachelor of science (B.S.) tracks. Usually the B.A. track has fewer required courses in the major and is considered more of a general liberal arts degree. It is the degree typically chosen by students planning to go directly to graduate or professional school or by those who want the flexibility of choosing more electives outside their major field. The B.S. degree is preferred by employers seeking bachelor's-level candidates in math and science.

Use of Electives

Even with the number of courses students must take for their major, their minor (if they choose one), and the university requirements, they still have many electives from which to choose to achieve the required hours for graduation. Judicious use of these electives can make students both better educated and more marketable. We recommend that *all* students take courses in these six subjects:

- Basic writing (particularly business writing)
- Public speaking
- Computer literacy (word processing, desktop publishing, and spreadsheet software)

- Foreign language (a minimum of two years)

- Business or economics (a minimum of one to two courses)

- Accounting (one to three courses)

Some of these courses (e.g., accounting) may not be offered at all colleges or universities, or they may be difficult to obtain because space is reserved for majors only. Students can investigate alternative routes, such as enrolling at another institution close by (some neighboring schools even have agreements that allow students to do so at no additional cost), taking the course/s at a community college or at their own school in the summer (when access may be easier), taking the courses online or by correspondence, or enrolling in a summer business institute. (See Chapter 6.)

Students should select other electives according to their career plan in order to obtain the knowledge and skills for their field of interest and to add to their qualifications as a prospective employee (as discussed in Chapter I). Obviously, some electives should be chosen to explore other areas of interest.

Preparing For A Global Society

With virtually every large business, and many smaller ones as well, in the global marketplace, employers are emphasizing foreign language skills and international and intercultural experience as never before. Languages currently most in demand by employers are Spanish, Russian, Portuguese, and Asian and Middle-Eastern languages. Knowledge of one foreign language improves the ability to learn others; therefore, even if your child selected one language to study and later finds that a different one would have been better for his or her field, the time and effort learning the language will not have been wasted. Many graduate and professional schools also require, or at least value, foreign language skills.

Language skills alone, however, do not open many doors to jobs other than teaching. There are few opportunities to work strictly as a translator or interpreter, and native speakers or individuals who are proficiently bilingual (or multilingual) are usually sought to fill these. Knowledge of a language should be combined with other marketable skills.

International travel and study broaden students' horizons and help them develop fluency in a foreign language. International experience and language skills can be especially helpful for some careers, like art history, archaeology, foreign language teaching, the travel industry, customer service, the Peace Corps, the Foreign Service, and government intelligence (e.g., FBI, CIA), and can give students an edge over other applicants. Nevertheless, candidates must have additional marketable skills in order to be in a strong position for entry-level employment.

Many students are so eager to travel abroad that they do so without fully considering the consequences of missing a semester on campus or a summer internship. Students interested in a semester abroad should make sure that they will not miss necessary courses offered only in the semester in which they are overseas. Also, students should avoid, if possible, being off-campus in their senior year, so that they will not miss campus interview opportunities. Summer travel is best done between the freshman and sophomore years, when students are less likely to be able to obtain significant work experience or internships. It is not advisable for students, especially juniors, to choose summer travel over an internship. Employers don't tend to look favorably on students who graduate without a job and spend months traveling before seeking employment.

Academic Honors

It is quite special for a student to be awarded academic honors. Academic scholarships, the Dean's List, university or department honors programs, and academic honorary societies and awards demonstrate that the student stands out among his or her peers in terms of academic achievement. These programs and awards challenge, stimulate, and motivate the superior student, and they are highly valued by many employers. Students who have the option to participate in honors programs and elect to do so should be aware, however, that the demands may be great in terms of time and effort.

Sometimes students who have earned honors don't realize that they should proudly claim them; in fact, they may dismiss opportunities to do so because they cost a minimal amount of money or effort. Jason, a sophomore at a costly private university, casually mentioned to his parents that he had received a letter of invitation for an honorary society of his major, speech, but chose not to join because it cost $30. His parents quickly told him that they would gladly pay the fee and hoped it wasn't too late to do so. "Do you really think we wouldn't pay an extra $30 to allow you to claim an honor which you've worked so hard for?" they asked him. Jason hadn't thought about the value of being a member of an academically elite group and also of being able to list the honor on his résumé later.

A Wall Street Journal article described the case of a college alumnus who had not responded to an invitation to join Phi Beta Kappa. More than a decade after graduation, learning how prestigious it was among his peers, he called his alma mater to see whether it was too late to become a member. It wasn't, and he joined, adding it to his résumé. Honoraries typically require a one-time membership fee for lifetime benefits, including regular publications, opportunities for networking, fellowships, etc.

As desirable as academic achievement is, though, high grades and honors without work experience, leadership roles, and marketable skills will not prepare today's graduates to be competitive in the job market.

How Parents Can Help

It is important for you to listen to your son or daughter's thoughts about choosing a major. Some students want to talk with their parents frequently about their major or career, while others don't want to think about or discuss these issues. In either case, try to be patient and supportive. Encourage open discussion about why your son or daughter is considering a particular major and what he or she hopes to accomplish by choosing it. Help your child think through issues such as course options and requirements, academic demands, reputation of the department, and relevance to career goals.

Students may have some anxiety about making these important decisions. Many seem to choose a major by waiting until the last possible moment and then throwing a dart at a list of majors offered. Assure your child that the decision is not irrevocable. What is key is that he or she not procrastinate about exploring the issues and gathering information to make an informed decision.

Keep in mind that students differ widely in their readiness to make decisions about their major and career and that most students will change their major at least once. Raise questions and concerns in a non-judgmental way, showing your interest in helping your child make the best decision *for him or her* and one that will aid in achievement of his *or her* goals.

Summary

....

Factors to Consider When Selecting a Major

- Students should major in a subject they enjoy

- Students should major in something in which they can do well

- Parents should not worry if the major isn't career-related (but encourage their student to develop and follow through on a career plan)

Minors/Interdisciplinary Major

- Students can "construct their own major" through use of a major plus a minor or through an interdisciplinary major

Double Majors

- Students may double-major for specific career or personal goals

- Double majors aren't generally valued by employers unless they specifically relate to the employer's needs

Use of Electives

Students should choose electives:

- To explore possible majors

- To gain marketable skills

- To enhance their qualifications

- According to their career goals and plan

Importance of Grades

High grades are usually necessary for:

- Employment related to math, chemistry, physics, accounting, and engineering

- Careers such as consulting and investment banking

- Graduate/professional school admission

Most employers seek new graduates with a 3.0 or higher GPA

Role of Honors

- Students should strive to attain academic honors

- Students should join academic honorary organizations if they qualify

- Honors are impressive to most employers

- Honors and high grades without work experience, leadership roles, and marketable skills aren't sufficient to lead to employment

Helping Your Child

- Encourage open communication about majors and careers

- Not be judgmental about the student's choices

- Be patient and supportive, but raise important questions and issues

Conversation Starters for Parents and Students

1. Which college classes have you enjoyed the most? Why?

2. When do you have to declare a major?

Choosing a Major: Drama versus Accounting

3. Have you talked with your academic adviser and a counselor in the career office about choosing a major? What was their advice?

4. Which majors are you considering? Why these?

5. Do you think you are likely to do well academically in the major you are considering?

6. Which major or majors do you think would best prepare you for your career goals?

7. Which electives do you think would best complement your major?

CHAPTER 4

HOW LONG SHOULD IT TAKE?

....

"So, have you started to think about your plans after graduation next year? Tom O'Reilly looked hopefully at his son Robert, a college junior.

"I think I'm going to need more time. Hardly anybody graduates in four years these days. It doesn't look like I have enough credits to finish next year. Besides, I'm thinking of getting a double major. I might be able to do it in four and a half years, five at the most," Robert replied.

....

While some students push themselves to graduate early, others aren't in any hurry to finish their bachelor's degree. How long *should* it take?

Not surprisingly, parents and their children often have different perspectives on the length of time needed to complete college. Parents generally assume that less is more. While they spend less money for tuition, living expenses, and books, their son or daughter earns more income by beginning full-time employment sooner. Less time in college seems even more advantageous if a student is contemplating graduate or professional school. Finally, let's not overlook the bragging potential of telling all of their friends that their child is graduating in "only three years."

Students, on the other hand, may not be in any hurry to leave college for the real world, with all its uncertainties. They may want to take a light load to keep their grades as high as possible, to squeeze in many extracurricular activities, or simply to allow for an active social life.

There is no one answer that is right for every student. Graduating early (in less than four years) is not necessarily good, nor is graduating late (in more than four years) necessarily bad. In making that decision, it is important to consider your son or daughter's particular situation and goals, as well as the advantages and disadvantages of graduating "off schedule".

Graduating Early

....

Susan, a college senior, looked down at the draft of her résumé with disbelief. It looked so skimpy, somehow.

Her college career counselor prompted her optimistically, "What about work experience—internships, summer jobs, or part-time employment? Have you done any volunteer work or been involved in any extracurricular activities?"

"No. No. No. I didn't have time because I'm finishing in three years."

"I see," remarked the counselor, confident that there was surely something that Susan had forgotten to list on her résumé and that he would help her find it. "What about academic honors, such as the Dean's List?"

"Yes, but only once," Susan conceded. Although she was a top student in high school, her college transcript was respectable but not exceptional.

....

Some students speed through college as if in a race against time, completing a bachelor's degree in as little as two and a half to three years. Why do they graduate so quickly and how do they do it?

Why Students Graduate Early

College Preparatory Classes

Some students who take college-level classes in high school do not expect to need the traditional four years to complete a bachelor's degree. If they don't feel sufficiently challenged by their course work, they may graduate early. These students have often been academically gifted from an early age. They–and their parents–assume that if it takes most college student four years to graduate, surely *they* can do it in less time.

Advanced Placement, Dual Enrollment, and International Baccalaureate

Very bright students often begin college with a head start; they pass advanced placement (AP) tests or enter with credits obtained at a local college while enrolled in high school.

Students may "place out" of nearly two semesters of college work. However, if they enroll in a course beyond the introductory one, they may find that they missed an important concept that is key to their understanding the material. This can be especially problematic in courses required for a student's major; therefore, we do not recommend that a student place out of courses in the major, even if they are eligible to do so.

Scores on advanced placement tests range from 1-5, with most colleges granting credit for students who score from 3-5. Some institutions are starting to accept scores as low as 2. According to the College Board, most students with a score of 4-5 performed "extremely well" in subsequent classes compared to those who took the prerequisite course.

First-year students enrolled in upper-level courses are competing for grades with juniors and seniors while adjusting to college life as freshmen. The first year of college is usually difficult for students. High school valedictorians are now classmates. Good grades may not come as easily as they once did: parents are not close by to ensure good study habits; there are more distractions than in high school; competition is stiffer; and classes may be bigger and more impersonal. Many college seniors express embarrassment about a GPA that doesn't reflect their ability. If they took advanced level courses as a freshman, they regret not asking questions of a professor during his or her office hours, saying that they felt "intimidated," while juniors and seniors in the same class were comfortable requesting help.

A computer science professor at a major university says that he can always tell which students have been granted AP credit to skip the first one or two levels of calculus. He says that there is no comparison between a calculus course taught by a high school teacher and one led by a mathematician with a Ph.D. Students may have learned enough to pass the AP test but have no idea how to apply calculus to scientific problems. "It is a very rare 18-year-old who has the intellectual maturity to succeed in upper-level college courses. Unfortunately, they often receive low grades and conclude that they don't have the potential to succeed in majors (and future careers) that require a high degree of mathematics skill."

Successfully passed AP tests count toward credit hours; however, grades on these tests are not factored into a student's GPA. Again, this may be a disadvantage that accompanies the head start on college. Instead of receiving A's in introductory courses, a student may earn Bs and Cs in higher-level courses. The former high school valedictorian may not even qualify for the Dean's List, despite high expectations.

Students who use AP credits to enter college with sophomore status may not graduate early after all. Instead, they take a light course load of 12 hours instead of 15 hours and graduate with their entering class. After studying hard in high school to get into a good college, they feel entitled to take it easy and enjoy a more active social life.

According to the associate registrar at a Florida university, students who earn poor grades in dual enrollment programs could be placed on probation or suspension or be dismissed by the end of freshman year. Students who took college-level courses while in high school don't seem to understand that their college transcript started at that time. Other complications may occur. For example, Jessica intended to major in nursing and received college credit while in high school with a grade of C- for a biology course. She later discovered that nursing majors may not receive less than a C in a prerequisite course. She also learned that a different biology course was required for health majors and so the one she had taken in high school would not have counted towards her nursing degree, even if she had earned a higher grade.

Heavy Course Loads

A student may accelerate college by taking more credit hours than average (possibly 18-21 hours per semester as opposed to 12-15). Grades may suffer, though, with less study time available for each class. In addition, a heavy course load may preclude or decrease involvement in extracurricular activities and part-time employment. Since many courses have prerequisites, early graduation may also limit a student's options for electives, since all courses are not offered each term. (Some students take a few courses through correspondence or an online university, although they need to ensure that the institution is accredited and that the credits will transfer to their college.)

Summer School

Malcolm, a college senior, had never held a job, which surprised his career counselor. Even with a 3.6 GPA in computer science, the lack of practical experience would be noticed by recruiters. "What did you do with your summers?" the counselor asked. Malcolm replied, "I went to summer school, traveled abroad, and babysat for my younger sister."

Students attending summer school for two or three summers may be able to graduate at least one or two terms early. These students may complete college without any work experience, putting themselves at a disadvantage, since employers place increasing importance on experience related to a student's career goals. Summer internships provide valuable experience for students who are available for work. As an alternative, students attending summer school several summers should obtain career-related experience during the school year through part-time jobs, volunteer work, or other sources. "Virtual" internships (that is, performing work for an employer from a remote location) may be possible for students, such as designing a website from a residence hall for a nonprofit organization. (See Chapter 5.)

Graduate School Plans

Students sometimes regard a bachelor's degree as merely a necessary prelude to graduate school. Why not speed things up, they reason. The more quickly they can complete their undergraduate studies, the sooner they can begin graduate work. For some students this reasoning is sound; they save time and a substantial amount of money. Others, however, experience burnout and decide to take time off before continuing their studies. They may find themselves drifting for a year or two, unable to obtain significant work because they have little more to present to employers than high grades.

Some universities offer qualified students the opportunity to combine an undergraduate with a graduate or professional school degree. For example, a business major may be able to combine his senior year with his first year of MBA work, resulting in a savings of one academic year and a significant amount of tuition money, and the opportunity to begin working one year earlier than most MBAs. Or, a pre-med student may be able to enroll in medical school after only three years of undergraduate education.

Financial Savings

The cost of a college education can run over $130,000 at private institutions and $40,000 at public ones (particularly for out-of-state students). Students may rush through their academic work for financial reasons. Several colleges have initiated special programs to allow students to graduate in three years or less and have predicted tuition savings of up to $30,000. Some colleges offering a three year bachelor's degree are Ball State University, Clarkson University, and East Carolina University. In addition to financial savings, these students receive priority in registering for courses and have a designated academic advisor to facilitate graduation in three years.

East Carolina University is one of the universities that allow qualified students to "Succeed Sooner". Undergraduates with Advanced Placement, International Baccalaureate or dual-enrollment credit may apply to earn a "Degree in Three," and begin graduate-level studies before completing their bachelor's degree. The program offers Graduate Study Connections, which can decrease by one year the amount of time required for a master's in education, or a degree in medicine, law, optometry, dentistry, and optometry. (Graduate level courses in the senior year count toward both undergraduate and graduate degrees.)

Impact of Graduating Early

Prospective employers and graduate and professional schools have mixed reactions to early graduation. On the one hand, it is an accomplishment and shows commitment to a difficult goal; on the other, however, students may sacrifice academic honors, work experience, and extracurricular and volunteer activities, which contribute to their maturity level and qualifications.

Employers usually ask students *what they accomplished* during college, not *how quickly they graduated*. Recruiters who are seeking students with superior quantitative skills may ask to see their transcript to look at grades in math-related courses. Students who have placed out of mathematics and have not taken higher-level math/quantitative courses have more difficulty demonstrating their ability (although they can do it by showing high quantitative SAT or GRE scores). For some students graduating early is a good choice. For others it is not. Early graduation requires trade-offs that students should weigh carefully.

Graduating Late

··

B.J. said, "My parents told me that I should ask you about the best time to graduate. I'll be a fifth-year senior next fall and will have enough credits to graduate in December, but could take some additional courses and wait for May. Plus I've heard that May is a better time to graduate."

··

Most students are not quite this candid about their reluctance to end their college years and enter the real world; however, their misgivings are evident. Fear of failure is one reason. Inertia may overtake students, whose lives have been circumscribed by class schedules for 16 to 17 years of school and college.

Only 53 percent of college students nationwide graduate in four years, (The figure is 48% percent for students in public institutions and 67 percent for those in private schools.) The two primary causes for delays in graduation are limited financial aid, which drives students to combine work and school, and light course loads.

Why Students Graduate Late

Light Course Loads

Students at colleges on the semester system generally need to take an average of 15 credit hours each term (excluding summers) to graduate in four years. Increasingly, students are choosing course loads lighter than 15 hours–at least some semesters–and are graduating later as a result.

There are several reasons for a student's decision to take fewer courses: to allow time for employment in order to earn money to finance college expenses or to obtain related experience; to increase study time to improve grades; or to participate in extracurricular activities or volunteer activities.

A job related to a student's career goals could be ideal and add to a student's credentials. For example, a pre-med student attended training at a community college and became a Certified Emergency Medical Technician, working part-time in the health field while paying for college costs. A medical school may be impressed with this student's ability to work under pressure with patients of various ages and medical conditions.

For students who struggle financially, the highest paying part-time job may seem to be the answer, whether or not it is related to their ultimate career aspirations. A job as a server in a fine restaurant may allow flexible hours and provide a student the opportunity to make more money in tips than an hourly job. As an alternative to trying to juggle work and classes, some students drop out of college for one term or more to work and save money for college expenses. This option also results in delayed graduation.

Students may take a light course load in an attempt to increase their GPA, since they have more study time for each class. Although their grades may rise, some academic honors (such as the Dean's List or Phi Beta Kappa) require higher qualifying grades for students taking fewer hours. As a result, some students maintain a good GPA but do not have the academic honors normally associated with it. Recipients of the University of Georgia's merit-based HOPE Scholarships, who must maintain at least a 3.0 GPA to retain their financial assistance, have been found to take fewer courses at a time and to drop difficult classes more often than other students.

Some students take a light course load to fulfill their commitment to demanding extracurricular or volunteer activities. Certain leadership positions, such as student body president or editor of the student newspaper, require nearly as many hours as a full-time job. Students may spend just as much time in volunteer activities, often career related, such as tutoring underprivileged children, political campaigns, ,and social activism. Varsity sports commonly demand 30 or more hours a week for practice, games, and travel.

Other students start the term with a full class load but drop one or two of their courses. Although there are valid reasons for dropping a class, students often bail out at the first sign of boredom or difficulty. The result, of course, is a light load, which delays graduation and might be awkward to explain to a potential employer reviewing a student's transcript. At some universities course that are dropped late will appear on the transcript, raising further questions from employers or graduate school admissions officers.

Academic Reasons

Students may find their graduation delayed because admission tests reveal they need remedial course work. Remedial classes do not count toward graduation requirements. In addition, students at some institutions are allowed to repeat courses to make better grades, which could prevent them from graduating on schedule. Transfer students sometimes lose course credits when they enroll in a different institution, which also prolongs their college stay.

Many colleges are experiencing financial difficulties and have chosen to decrease the number of course they offer. Students may have difficulty obtaining the courses needed for their major or as prerequisites for graduation; their graduation may be delayed until they are able to enroll in the necessary courses.

Your child should look ahead and outline a four-year course plan for his or her desired major. (Although the plan will probably change, it will be a good starting point.) He or she should determine which courses are required, and in which sequence, and try to enroll in them as early as possible. If unable to enroll, your child should consider alternatives: investigating whether the course is offered at a neighboring institution and, if so, whether the credits will transfer; discussing the situation with his or her academic adviser or academic dean to learn if there is any way to enroll in the class; or talking with the class instructor to see if there is some flexibility in the size of the class or if any students have dropped the class since he or she tried to enroll.

As emphasized in Chapter 3, many students change majors several times during their college years. If the former major is very different from the new one—as, for example, with a switch from English to biology—the student may need additional time to complete core courses and related electives. Students may want to consider continuing in the current major and adding a minor or electives in the new area of interest if changing majors will delay graduation. This is especially true if the student is an upperclassman and the new major is not directly career related.

Some colleges report that more students are choosing to double major as they try to differentiate themselves from their classmates for very selective jobs or graduate schools. Up to 40% of students at Boston University have more than one major, compared to 5% at Harvard and 15% at Yale. In addition to double majors, Northeastern University offers "integrated dual majors," approved combinations of majors that require several "capstone" courses that help students to apply knowledge from two disciplines. Although some colleges allow some overlap, with courses applying to more than one major, it's not unusual for students to tell their career advisors, "With just four more courses I could get another major."

Increasingly more majors, such as accounting, pharmacy, and some engineering disciplines, require five or six years to complete. Also, universities may either require or strongly encourage students in particular majors, like engineering, to participate in cooperative education programs, generally resulting in an extra semester or two. Students in these programs are not actually graduating late, but they will not, of course, graduate in four years.

Study abroad may also lengthen the time to graduate, since courses taken at a foreign university may not all transfer, and students may miss required courses that are offered only once a year.

Students may receive poor academic advising and not realize that they are missing courses required for graduation. Many colleges provide a checklist to help students ensure that they have the right combination of courses and credit hours necessary to graduate in their major.

Slow Maturation

Although students would be loath to admit it, many use college as a time to "find themselves." If they don't have a career direction as their senior year approaches, they are fearful of graduating and being at a loss for what to do next. Hence they prolong college by taking "just a few more courses" in hopes of finding a career focus or feeling ready to leave the cocoon of the college environment.

Impact of Graduating Late

Employers sometimes evaluate late graduation negatively. They believe it may reveal a lack of motivation, poor planning, or academic problems. Late graduation is more obvious when a student finishes a degree in December or the summer. A five-year degree may go without notice if the student is graduating in May. However, a student should be prepared with an explanation if interviewers ask about the reasons for late graduation.

Although students may believe they have good reasons to delay graduation, parents are also interested in the economic impact. The "opportunity cost" of graduating late includes tuition and fees, books, and foregone income during any extra terms. Students who take an extra term and graduate in December instead of May or June could lose more than $23,000, assuming college costs of $6,000 for one additional term and foregone wages of $2,500 for seven months. In addition, some universities charge more per credit hour for those exceeding the number needed to graduate.

Some students assume that parental financial support will last indefinitely. Parents should inform students early if the family budget for education is available for a specific length of time, such as four years.

Best Months to Graduate

According to a survey conducted by the University of North Carolina at Chapel Hill, employers prefer to hire college students who graduate in May and December. Recruiters ranked June third and August last. Large organizations, such as Fortune 500 corporations or federal government agencies, schedule their management trainee programs to begin when most college students graduate. Students completing their studies "out of sync" may find that they have to wait for the next training program.

For an August graduate the delay for a job or additional studies (most graduate and professional schools begin in the fall) could be four to five months. It may be difficult for an August graduate to find meaningful short-term employment while waiting to enter graduate school or to begin a "real" job. Employers may assume that highly qualified students will not remain available and therefore not consider them for employment.

Bottom Line

....

It is obvious that there is no one answer that is right for all students concerning time to graduate. In many situations involving late graduation, there is little, if any, choice. We suggest that you frequently discuss with your son or daughter his or her academic plans and progress, closely examining the advantages, disadvantages, and likely consequences of each decision. We also recommend consulting with the college's academic and career advisers about these decisions and their impact.

Summary

....

Graduating Early

Possible Advantages

- Money saved on tuition

- Graduation at younger age

- Earlier graduate/professional school start

- Earlier career/employment start

Possible Disadvantages

- Low grades

- Fewer opportunities to take electives (either for enhancing marketability or expanding education)

- Less time for leadership roles, volunteer work

- Less time for personal growth and maturation

- Less time for summer/part-time work experience, internships, etc.

Most Appropriate Candidates

- Students with very limited financial support

- Students with excellent grades and who are planning immediately to enter lengthy graduate/professional programs (e.g., medical, dental, veterinary, law school; Ph.D. programs)

- Students with good to excellent grades planning to enter high-demand careers requiring little experience (e.g., nursing, pharmacy, math or science teaching)

Graduating Late

Possible Advantages

- More time for slow starters to ease into college and improve grades (by taking fewer classes)

- Chance for student to change major rather than graduate in an ill-fitting one

- More time to take extra courses of interest or to improve employability (e.g., electives in business, accounting, or computer science)

- More time to gain career-related work experience through cooperative education, internship programs, or part-time jobs

- More time to work to finance college education, perhaps avoiding high indebtedness with college loans

- More time for extracurricular, volunteer, and leadership activities

- More study time for each course (due to lighter course load), possibly resulting in higher grades

Possible Disadvantages

- Greater college costs

- Many employers and graduate schools prejudiced against students graduating in 4+ years

Most Appropriate Candidates

- Students transferring from other schools or changing majors

- Students in programs where 4+ years for graduation is the norm (e.g., pharmacy, accounting, engineering)

- Students taking lighter course loads to allow time for employment

- Students studying abroad

- Students needing to drop out of school for a term for personal, medical, or academic reasons

Conversation Starters for Parents and Students

....

1. How long does your major usually require for graduation?

2. How much time does your (extracurricular) activity and volunteer work take per week?

3. Have you considered summer school? Why or why not?

4. What do you think are the disadvantages of your graduating early or graduating late?

CHAPTER 5

GETTING EXPERIENCE AND MAKING CONTACTS

Three Résumés

Kathryn Johnson, a recruiter for a consumer products company, looks at the stack of over a hundred résumés from the university where she will recruit next month for sales representatives. She represents a company that is very selective. Her employer recruits from only 28 universities nationwide, a decrease from 90 schools three years ago.

Ms. Johnson will consider students with any major for these openings, but competitive applicants must have leadership skills, a sincere interest in sales, a high energy level, and a record of setting and achieving goals. They must also be well-rounded team players. Grades are not a major factor, but candidates must have at least a 2.8 GPA, preferably a 3.0. The job pays $40,000 a year to start, and students consider the company to be a prestigious employer. The first three résumés Ms. Johnson reviews reflect the difference in students' backgrounds.

Résumé 1: Brandon

Brandon, an economics major, has a 2.5 GPA. The glee club appears to be his only activity on campus. He held a part-time job for one year shelving books in the library and worked one summer as a lifeguard and another as a waiter.

Résumé 2: Laura

Laura majored in history and minored in Spanish. She has a 2.9 GPA and was on the Dean's List one semester. Her activities include volunteer work as a Big Buddy to an underprivileged child, intramural volleyball, and membership on the social committee for her residence hall. Her résumé cites courses in public speaking, accounting, and marketing.

Laura has spent her last three summers as a sales clerk in a department store, as a camp counselor, and as head camp counselor (a promotion).

Part-time jobs as a waitress and as a receptionist helped her earn 40% of her college expenses. She lists computer skills such as Microsoft Word, Excel, Access, and PowerPoint.

Résumé 3: Trent

Trent majored in English and minored in business. His GPA is 3.2, and he has been on the Dean's List three semesters. His résumé states his objective: "A position as a sales representative with opportunities for advancement."

The rest of Trent's résumé is consistent with an interest in sales. One section is labeled "Related Courses" and lists marketing, consumer behavior, and advertising. Another heading is "Related Experience" and lists jobs as a sales associate in a men's clothing store, a sales representative for college telephone directories (in which he sold ad space to businesses), and a promotion to sales team leader for the same firm. He also had a marketing internship with a nonprofit organization, adding information and advanced features to its website.

Trent also developed his persuasive skills through serving as a rush chairman for his fraternity (recruiting new members), as fund-raiser for the university development office (making calls to alumni to solicit donations), and as campaign manager for a student body president candidate. In addition, he is captain of his intramural basketball team. He has extensive computer skills and is proficient in Spanish.

Career Planning and Career Competition

You can see why competition is keen for management trainee positions. If a recruiter sees many résumés like Trent's, other candidates pale in comparison. Trent is representative of students who select a career interest early and do effective career planning.

Like most students, Trent didn't *begin* college with a burning desire to pursue sales as a career. He needed a part-time job, and retail sales positions were easy to find. A friend recruited Trent to join the rush committee of his fraternity. Since he enjoyed both of these activities and was successful in them, Trent decided to look for other opportunities to use his persuasive skills and to target sales as a career.

Laura's résumé goes into the "maybe" pile. It would have been easier for her to compete for job openings several years ago, when entry-level jobs were more plentiful and fewer students obtained career-related experience prior to graduation. Even if her background is not targeted enough for this employer, it may be attractive to retailers and non-profits.

Ms. Johnson spends little time on Brandon's résumé. There are many students like him. They may have an active social life in college and do not put much effort into their studies. Their families may not expect them to help finance their education and do not make work a priority for their college student. Some students attend summer school or travel during semester breaks and are not available for work. Regardless of the reasons, students like Brandon will find it difficult to obtain interviews with prospective employers. If he's lucky, a family member or other contact is employed at an organization and will put in a good word for him, resulting in a "courtesy interview." If it goes well, he may receive serious consideration despite his lack of credentials.

Students without focus or experience will need to work harder at the job search. Since on-campus interviews are so competitive, they will need to be especially assertive in obtaining interviews from off-campus. (See Chapter 9.) After graduation they may need to begin at a low-level position, such as customer service representative or bank teller, to prove themselves first and then apply for promotion from within the organization to a management training program or enter a business institute program. (See Chapter 6.) Another option is to find an unpaid internship after graduation to develop marketable skills and make contacts.

Many students find their niche through trial and error and are still able to develop impressive backgrounds by graduation. Beth entered college as an engineering major but did not find her classes interesting. As a result of her summer job in a manufacturing plant, she became fascinated with the emphasis on lean manufacturing (eliminating waste and inefficiency). She decided to change her major to business and concentrated in production management. Her engineering background is an asset in this field in which fewer work hours, less inventory, shorter product development time, and lower space requirements result in increased profit.

You want your child to have the best possible preparation for his or her future career. This chapter will give some ideas about ways for your son or daughter to obtain career-related experience and marketable skills.

Internships

....

Marketability to Employers

Large corporations have fewer openings for new college graduates than in the past as a result of downsizing, reorganization, and automation. They can afford to be highly selective. Internships and other career-related experiences are becoming increasingly important. Vault, Inc reports that about 75% of college students obtain an internship. More than half (55%) of internships are estimated to be unpaid. A recent survey by the National Association of Colleges and Employers found that employers offered approximately half of their interns and co-ops full-time jobs, about two-thirds of which were accepted.

It is not unusual for employers to interview students with multiple job-related internships, part-time jobs, and extracurricular or volunteer activities. These candidates have a competitive advantage. Employers are reluctant to take a risk on unfocused, inexperienced students when training and turnover costs are so high. One Fortune 500 company reported investing about $150,000 on management trainees during their first year with the company. College students used to be hired for their potential. Today they need proven skills. Former interns have been tested, according to recruiters. Internship experience also provides students with polish and business savvy so that they adjust more quickly to a first job after college.

The most competitive employers target students with experience in the same industry. One investment banking recruiter expresses a preference for students with an internship with a national or regional investment bank. Also acceptable, he says, is experience with a major commercial bank, brokerage firm, or Fortune 500 company.

Definition of an Internship

An internship differs from a summer or part-time job in that an internship consists of career-related work rather than such duties as typing, filing, waiting on tables, or operating a cash register. The internship role can be compared to an apprenticeship. It may include assisting a professional with day-to-day activities or completing special project assignments. Every intern can expect to perform some clerical or routine duties, but these activities should not constitute the bulk of the student's time.

Students perform internships in industries as diverse as entertainment, stockbrokerage, health care, retailing, law, and government. Examples of internship employers and the positions they offer include *Time* magazine (marketing), the Spoleto Festival (media relations, orchestra management), and the National Institutes of Health (technology transfer and licensing).

Some organizations offer internships abroad. A study abroad program, Internships in Europe, matches students with unpaid internships related to their career interests. Other sources of overseas internships include Intern Abroad, Global Experiences, and International Internships. About half of the internships offered by the U.S. Department of State are in embassies and consulates in other countries.

Virtual Internships

After demonstrating skills and good work habits, an employer may allow a student intern to work from college and submit the work electronically rather than report to the employer's location.

Ted, a freshman in computer science, worked part-time during the school year for a fast-growing software firm. During the summer he continued his job as a full-time summer intern from his hometown across the state.

Some nonprofit organizations post virtual internships on their website or on the website of various college career centers. Students may work part-time from their dorm room (or hometown!) to design websites, research potential funding sources, edit newsletters, and perform graphic design, among other tasks. These positions may be paid or unpaid.

Benefit of Internships

"Reality-testing" is an important feature of internships. An internship can provide exposure to a career field, industry, and employer without the pressure of making a long-term commitment. Your son may not have realized that advertising was so fast-paced. Or, a student may find that human resources involves more than recruiting and training functions and that salary and benefits administration are not as appealing after first-hand exposure.

The internship experience can enable your child to use and enhance current skills and develop new ones. In some cases, assignments may result in tangible work samples for your child to show prospective employers: for example, a PowerPoint presentation with special effects, an interactive website, or written articles for a company newsletter. An internship will stand out on a senior's résumé, particularly if it is related to a career goal. Since many organizations use internships as a recruiting source, your child is likely to have an "edge" when being considered by the internship employer for a full-time job.

An internship can result in a higher salary offer later. A poll by Coopers and Lybrand found that about half of the 187 employers they surveyed offered a salary premium to recent college graduates with work experience such as internships. Your son or daughter's salary offer as a senior may be $100-200 a month higher than their peers' who did not hold an internship. Former interns may also be promoted more quickly as a result of their experience.

Internships can serve as stepping-stones to contacts and future opportunities. Students in an internship program may meet company executives and receive more visibility than a larger group of management trainees. In addition to their co-workers, students may work with customers or clients, suppliers, and so on. All of these contacts become potential networking connections for job leads. Also, students learn many job search skills while seeking an internship: writing a résumé, preparing cover letters, networking with contacts, completing applications, and interviewing for openings. Former interns have a head start senior year when they look for regular employment.

How do employers benefit by offering internships? They supplement their staff with eager and talented young people who may be considered for future employment. Some interns have learned state-of-the-art techniques on campus and bring new ideas to an organization. Students sometimes make contributions for which they are long remembered. The Federal Reserve Bank of Minneapolis named its electronic bulletin board Kimberley, after a summer intern who designed the system in 1989!

Internship Goal-Setting

Your child may say, "I want to find an internship," yet need help in thinking through his or her goals. Goals could include testing an interest in one of several career fields, developing specific skills, and making contacts. For example, a student may wish to explore graphic arts as a career, upgrade skills with computer graphics and desktop publishing software, and develop contacts in Atlanta. The college's career office can help with this goal-setting process.

RÉSUMÉ-BUILDING INTERNSHIPS

What do interns **do**? You might be surprised at the diversity of their positions and the amount of responsibility they are given. Here are excerpts from the résumés of some students with internship experience.

Planning Intern-Business major

- Taught computer skills to ten managers and planning department professionals

- Developed Excel model to quote delivery dates for an experimental product line, using complicated macro and statistical formulas

Film Intern-Radio/TV/Motion Picture major

- Studied film production on the sets of films at Universal Studios, Amblin Entertainment, and Warner Brothers

Brokerage Intern-Business major

- Performed evaluations of post-bankruptcy companies, closed-end funds, corporate insider trading, and corporate spin-offs

Computer Support Intern-Mathematical Science major

- Created, updated, and modified databases using Access

Congressional Intern-Political Science major

- Briefed congressional offices on pending legislation

Investment Banking Summer Analyst-Business major

- Analyzed company financial data, built models, databases, and company profiles

Business Development Intern-Economics major/Japanese minor

- Developed wireless application revenue models from Asia for American market

News Room Intern-Journalism/Speech Communications major

- Wrote wire stories for the Associated Press

Industrial Engineering Co-op-Industrial Engineering major

- Developed flowchart for the production process of circuit boards to calculate failure rates, determine bottlenecks, and reduce lead times

Health Care Intern-Health Policy/Administration major

- Aided in developing recruitment plan for physical therapy department

Legal Intern-History major

- Located and interrogated witnesses in preparation for trial

Marketing Research Intern-Computer Science major

- Gathered information from prospective customers for telephone, automotive, and textile corporations

Research Assistant-Biology major

- Configured quantitative data for interpretation of results in published scientific article

Dolphin Research Assistant-Zoology major

- Compared mother/calf dolphin feeding activities to determine whether behavior is learned vs. instinctive

Credit Analyst Intern-Economics major

- Calculated and analyzed cash flow coverage

Public Policy Intern-Administration of Criminal Justice major

- Analyzed issues and prepared briefing books for decision makers

Engineering Intern- Electrical Engineering major

- Prepared engineering studies based on statistical and equipment data

Actuarial Intern-Actuarial Science major

- Created and analyzed management reports for Benefits Division

Internship Job Search

Once your child determines goals and parameters for the internship, it's time to begin searching for organizations to contact. The career office is likely to maintain resources such as *The Internship Bible, Vault Guide to Top Internships,* and *Internships 2006* to help identify prospective employers. Because these internships are widely publicized, applicants face heavy competition from the many other students who also have access to the listings. Some students apply to several hundred employers in order to secure an internship.

In addition to printed materials, the career office may have a service through which they mail résumés of students seeking internships to employers who list openings. Some employers also conduct on-campus interviews to recruit interns; however, most students find their positions through more informal methods such as networking.

Internships at some organizations may be targeted for minority students or technical majors. Also, some organizations offer internships and summer jobs to employees' children and rarely offer them to others. As a parent, you can check with your employer's human resources department to see whether such opportunities are available. Also, consider possibilities with a family business. Students often assume higher-level responsibilities when they work for a parent, aunt, or brother-in-law.

Students may create their own internships through networking with relatives, friends of the family, neighbors, faculty, and other sources. Initiative and assertiveness can pay off. One accounting student approached a recruiter from a small bank at a college career fair and convinced him that she would be a valuable intern. The recruiter was so impressed with her that he created an internship position for her that she held for two summers. The bank offered her a job when she graduated!

Most formal internship programs target students the summer between their junior and senior years. First year students usually find their opportunities to obtain internships are limited. They may need to volunteer for part-time internships during the school year and take summer jobs that are less career-related but nevertheless allow them to start acquiring skills and building their résumé. Some employers want an intern who can work for two summers, opening up possibilities for sophomores.

Next, your child needs to identify the factors to be considered in an internship search. Will he or she need a part-time internship so as to also attend summer school? Does he or she need to earn money, or is an unpaid internship possible? Are there geographic limitations to consider or is relocation or commuting an option? Some employers provide or subsidize housing for students who are working temporarily and may find it difficult to find short-term accommodations. Internships are often difficult to obtain, and your child should be as flexible as possible. Geographic mobility and willingness to accept unpaid internships will increase possible choices.

We can imagine what you are thinking: "But I want my child to return home for the summer." Especially if your son or daughter attends college away from home, you look forward to this time. However, experience in another city may be instrumental in opening future opportunities to work in his or her chosen field after graduation. You may need to sacrifice some of your own needs to help your child make a decision about internship opportunities.

Employers often prize evidence of a student's adaptability. If a position requires travel or relocation, recruiters are sometimes reluctant to hire students who have not worked, traveled, or studied outside their home state. Students from small towns or rural areas may find it especially difficult to compete for openings in large metropolitan areas like New York City or Chicago; employers believe that these candidates may be unable to adjust to such a different environment. A student's internship in a metropolitan area or study abroad may reassure prospective employers.

Academic Credit for Internships

Your child should check on his or her college's policy on receiving academic credit for internships. Some schools allow students to be paid for an internship *and* receive credit; others do not permit an intern to receive both. Academic credit requirements for internships are usually demanding. Students may have to prepare a learning contract to specify their learning objectives for the experience. They may also need to keep a journal of their activities, prepare an annotated bibliography (a brief summary of information in the sources) about the field in which they work, and write a paper about their internship. Their supervisor will probably be asked to write a performance evaluation at the conclusion of the internship. Some colleges and universities have added career-related experience as part of the required curriculum.

Unpaid Internships

Your son tells you about an ideal internship. It sounds like the perfect opportunity, but you sense that it is almost too good to be true. In the next breath, he mentions that it is unpaid. You are skeptical. Why shouldn't he be paid for his efforts? And shouldn't he help finance his college expenses? If the internship is in another city, your concerns mount. This "opportunity" may actually *cost* you money if you have to pay for housing, food, and commuting costs, which would be minimal if he lived at home.

On the other hand, you realize that this type of internship may not be available in your city (for example, publishing or film work). Your son could spend another summer working at the coffee shop, but that will not increase his chances to work in his field when he graduates.

There is a way to compromise. Some students work by day in an unpaid internship and work at night or on weekends for pay. As another alternative, they may decide to work more hours at a paid job during the school year to compensate for their loss of income during the summer.

Internships for College Graduates

Some employers will consider new college graduates for internship openings. These positions are often unpaid, but they provide an opportunity for graduates to acquire marketable skills. Once interns prove their worth, they may be offered paid employment. Even if they do not receive a job offer, interns will gain experience and contacts, which often increase their chances of finding a paid position.

Externships

Many people who are familiar with the concept of internships may not have heard of *externships*. A student who is considering a particular occupation, such as banking, may find it helpful to observe someone on the job in that field. This short-term experience is called an externship, or job-shadowing.

An externship experience usually lasts from half-a-day to a week. Semester breaks are ideal for students to participate in externships. The career office may match students with alumni or other contacts for externships. Students may also arrange for this experience on their own through personal or information interview contacts. Although an externship often does not provide hands-on experience, it can be beneficial. Your child can observe many characteristics of a possible career field. An extern may seek answers to the following questions:

- What are the duties of the job?

- Is the pace high pressure or relaxed?

- Does the job involve heavy contact with other people, or is the work more solitary?

- Does the person in the job work regular hours or frequent overtime?

- Would I feel comfortable with the personalities of people in this job or department? Would I fit in?

- What is the environment like? Do people wear traditional business dress such as suits, or are they casually dressed? Is the workplace plushly decorated or austere?

Your son or daughter may decide after an externship that an occupation is not a good match after all and be spared a dissatisfying first job after college. A positive experience could reinforce a career interest and provide contacts for a future internship.

Students often mention externship experiences during job interviews and on graduate school applications as evidence of serious interest in a career field. Recruiters have said that they are impressed with students who have completed an internship, an externship, or an informational interview in the field for which they are applying. These applicants are more likely to have realistic expectations about the career and know whether they will enjoy it and perform well in it.

Self-Employment

Some students create their own opportunities for work experience through self-employment:

- They design, order, and sell T-shirts with unique slogans.

- They operate a lawn care or house-painting service.

- They provide roommate-matching services for students in apartments.

- They design and distribute customer newsletters for small businesses.

- They tutor students.

- They sell snacks at the beach during school breaks.

- They buy and sell items on e-Bay

Student entrepreneurs develop many skills, such as advertising and selling a product or service, negotiating or setting prices, ensuring customer satisfaction, ordering inventory or scheduling services, keeping records, and filing taxes. Many also recruit and supervise other students, developing leadership skills.

Employers are often impressed with the initiative, risk-taking, and work ethic of self-employed students, but too much entrepreneurial activity may raise a red flag. A recruiter may wonder whether a student can take direction as an employee. A recruiter may also be cautious about hiring a budding entrepreneur for a lengthy training program, in case the student's hidden agenda is future self-employment. Student entrepreneurs should plan to obtain experience as an employee in addition to working for themselves.

Students may obtain entrepreneurial experience on some campuses. Columbia Student Enterprises at Columbia University includes tutoring and translating, tour book publishing, and snack delivery, among other services.

Door-to-Door Sales

Many parents are alarmed to hear about their child's plans to spend the summer selling books (or other merchandise) door-to-door in a strange city on a commission basis. This opportunity may be labeled as an internship. Students are usually recruited by other students, who will supervise them as part of a sales team.

Students who have sold books earn an average of $8,000 during their first summer, according to one publisher. But this figure does not include students who drop out early (about three in ten). Many students experience homesickness, become disillusioned with selling, or tire of 75-hour work weeks. (Students are encouraged to make a sales presentation to a prescribed number of prospects a day to win a special award.)

Some students earn over $50,000 in three months, usually as "student managers" in their third or fourth summer with the company. They profit from their own sales as well as from the sales of their team members. These star performers give testimonials about large profits, exciting incentive trips, and personal rewards that resulted from their experience.

Successful students rave about their summers selling door-to-door. They speak of the experience as one that led to their increased confidence, self-discipline, and interpersonal skills. In addition, these students say that they are proud of running their own business (as an independent contractor) and living independently.

Parents are often skeptical about door-to-door sales. Many call the college career office with questions:

How safe is door-to-door sales?

Students are typically assigned to rural or suburban locations. Employers give them guidelines for determining how to approach sales prospects. Female students are usually cautioned not to enter a home with a man unless he is accompanied by his wife or children.

How will my child find a place to live in another state?

One company provides a list of local families willing to rent rooms to college students and a list of churches with other referrals.

Can my child sell enough to cover expenses and make any profit?

Some students find this experience very lucrative; however, it is possible for students to *lose* money if they do not keep their living expenses low and work enough hours. Those who quit may find it hard to find other work because summer positions are filled.

How do prospective employers evaluate this experience?

Some employers (especially those recruiting for sales representatives) actually *ask* career offices for a list of students who spent a summer selling books door-to-door for a particular publisher. Others are favorably impressed with the experience when they see it on a résumé. Recruiters state that these students are self-motivated, confident, and mature and have already proven themselves to have unusual perseverance.

If your child is interested in fields which are very difficult to enter, such as journalism, broadcasting, or investment banking, directly related experience would be more helpful than door-to-door sales.

What kind of training is provided?

Students receive training in sales techniques and product knowledge. Some employers provide excellent training–as much as a full week–which can give students useful skills.

Door-to-door sales is a lucrative, character-building experience for some students and a big disappointment for others. Your child should explore all the facts before making a decision. You can help by suggesting questions to ask about this type of opportunity (such as the ones listed above). Your child should also request a list of students who sold for the company the previous summer and contact them for further information.

Other commission opportunities for students include selling cutlery or fire extinguishers and painting houses in their home-town, making sales demonstrations to friends and relatives and asking for referrals to contact. Paint-contracting companies recruit students to solicit business painting residential houses; some of these students supervise others and gain leadership experience.

Most parents do not consider these independent contractor positions to pose as much risk as door-to-door sales in another state. However, all straight commission positions carry some risks, since they do not provide any guaranteed income; compensation is based on a percentage of sales.

The Invisible Curriculum

Importance to Employers

According to the National Association of Colleges and Employers, employers who were surveyed responded that they considered students' personal traits and skills more important to success on the job than their "domain knowledge" (knowledge related to their major). Some of these personal traits include adaptability, risk taking, and creativity; the skills included problem-solving, teamwork, decision-making, and oral and written communication.

Many employer interview questions probe for these personal traits and skills. A recruiter may say to a student, "Give me an example of a time you solved a difficult problem." Another question could be, "Tell me a story about a time you took a risk and failed at a project. What did you learn from this experience?"

Employers with management training programs typically target students whose extracurricular experiences show active involvement in campus student organizations. Students in these groups frequently encounter situations that require teamwork, conflict resolution, and other useful skills. An employer may ask questions that demonstrate how the applicant has made an impact in an extracurricular activity:

- Tell me about a time when you increased the efficiency of a process or activity.

- Think of a time you came up with an innovative or creative project.

- Describe an event or project that you planned from start to finish.

- Did you take any actions that show your persuasive skills, such as recruiting, fundraising or publicity?

Employers are especially interested in students who have leadership roles, which serve as a "proxy" for supervisory experience and help employers identify applicants with management potential. Most students have not had the opportunity to supervise others in a work setting, or their supervisory experience is limited to non-business settings in positions such as head lifeguard, head waitress, or senior camp counselor. Interviewers may ask questions to probe leadership effectiveness such as:

- Tell me about any obstacles or problems you helped the group to overcome.

- Give me an example of a time that an officer or committee chair was not performing well and how you handled the situation.

- Describe your biggest achievement as leader of this organization.

Extracurricular Activities as Experience

Extracurricular activities sometimes provide students with even more powerful skills than internships. Consider these examples, excerpted from students' résumés:

President, Student Union
- Chaired the Board of Directors, which controls a $450,000 annual budget for programming films, art exhibits, concerts, speakers, festivals, and other special events

Co-Chair, Student Symposium
- Planned and organized a two-day event for over 700 students, faculty, and executives
- Coordinated facilities and catering of three meals for all participants
- Supervised 85 volunteers on the Facilities Committee

Campus organizations are diverse, and students develop many skills through leadership roles. Students at large universities have literally hundreds of organizations from which to choose, such as student government; sororities, fraternities, and residence halls; sports teams; hobby groups; clubs for individual majors; professional associations; political and religious groups; community service organizations; and cultural groups. If none of the current organizations interest your child, he or she could become founder of a new group, demonstrating initiative and leadership skills.

If you have a daughter who is a future banker or financial management trainee, she may want to run for treasurer in a club, student professional organization, or sorority. Many student treasurers administer budgets which exceed $100,000. She could join student government and become an auditor for student organizations.

If you have a son who is a would-be advertising, marketing, or fund-raising professional, he will find many leadership positions or committees related to his career goals. He can serve as a chairperson or member of a publicity, fraternity membership, (recruiting), or philanthropy (fund-raising) committee. If he aspires to a career in college admissions, he can help recruit prospective students to campus. He can serve as a tour guide for high school students and their parents.

A budding performer or writer does not necessarily have to be a drama or music major to audition for plays and choral groups. Campuses often have student-run television stations, radio stations, newspapers, literary journals, and publications devoted to political or social commentary.

Is your child interested in a career in law? Many campuses have a student-administered honor code. Students serve as defense attorneys, prosecutors, and jury members for hearings in which peers are accused of cheating, plagiarism, or other offenses. This experience provides students with research, interviewing, and public speaking skills. Some campuses or college towns offer a mediation or dispute settlement center and train students as mediators. Prospective lawyers also frequently participate in student government or compete on a debate team.

A student who is interested in international work can volunteer as an English conversation partner for a foreign student or enroll in a study-abroad program. Some students volunteer to translate for hospital patients who do not speak English. Others seek part-time or summer jobs at import or export firms.

"Promotions" in Campus Organizations

Students learn about teamwork and organizational behavior through their campus involvement. In addition, they can be "promoted" to positions of more responsibility. Here is an excerpt that illustrates a student's progression from freshman to senior:

DELTA DELTA DELTA SORORITY

Treasurer of Pledge Class (Freshman Year)
- Collected and accounted for $2,500 raised for charity by pledge class

Assistant Treasurer (Sophomore Year)
- Managed individual member activities accounts

Treasurer (Junior Year)
- Coordinated membership dues payments
- Collected past due accounts

Vice President of Finance (Senior Year)
- Plan and implement $500,000 budget
- Maintain accountability of sorority's fiscal status
- Supervise and train treasurer

The next example shows how another student "paid his dues" before assuming more responsibility:

THE EXPONENT (campus newspaper)

Staff Writer (Freshman year)
- Wrote stories for University Desk.

Assistant Managing Editor (Sophomore year)
- Laid out inside pages, supervised production of business supplement

Editorial Writer (Junior year)
- Wrote two weekly editorials and a humor column

Associate Editor (Senior year)
- Write weekly editorials, edit columns, solicit artwork, supervise writers, lay out pages

---

The following box display provides examples of campus activities and volunteer work as they relate to marketable skills.

Leadership Skills

Student Attorney General-Judiciary Branch, Student Government
- Investigated over 100 honor code violations

Resident Assistant-College Residence Hall
- Enforced housing policies and regulations for 60 residents

Captain and Coach -Rugby Club
- Coached undefeated 2006 season, winning state championship

Air Force ROTC
- Supervised 80 cadets (freshmen-seniors)

Marketing Skills

Fundraiser-College Development Office
- Raised over $8,000 in 13 weeks

Volunteer Coordinator-Senate Campaign
- Recruited and supervised 40 college student volunteers

Account Executive-Student Newspaper
- Sold display advertising in a geographic territory

Quantitative Skills

Treasurer-Fraternity
- Administered and allocated $414,000 annual budget

Tutor-Service Organization
- Tutored high school students in beginning and intermediate algebra and calculus

Marketing Assistant, University Athletic Department
- Oversaw marketing and promotions for Field Hockey and Gymnastics Teams

---

Communication Skills

Reporter-Student Newspaper
- Wrote feature stories for special tabloids

Volunteer Writer-Non-Profit Agency
- Wrote press releases and public service announcements

Volunteer-Crisis Hot Line
- Responded to callers with concerns such as unplanned pregnancy, domestic violence, and depression

Research Assistant-Psychology Department
- Tested subjects in study on depression in women

Computer Skills

Computer Lab Assistant-Computer Science Department
- Provided programming and technical instruction for students

Student Software Engineer-Computer Science Department
- Designed and implemented a graphical user interface

Foreign Language Skills

Japanese Tutor-Self-Employed
- Tutored juniors and seniors in advanced-level Japanese

Volunteer Translator-University Medical Center
- Translated for Spanish-speaking patients

Teaching Skills

Tutor, Community Service Organization
- Taught English as a second language to Hispanic and Asian women

Sports activities

Employers associate many positive characteristics with students' participation in sports. These students are often assumed to have a high energy level and to be competitive, goal oriented, and disciplined.

115

Employers may have seen games in which athletes perform under pressure-as a whole stadium watches! In addition, many athletes receive valuable experience in public speaking as a result of media interviews. Team sports yield additional benefits as students learn teamwork skills.

Varsity sports may require long hours for training, travel, and competition. Employers usually take this into consideration when weighing a student athlete's grades and experience.

Your child doesn't need to be a varsity athlete to list sports activities on a résumé. Many employers also favorably evaluate involvement with intramural and club sports.

Religious, Political and Minority Organizations

Some campus or volunteer activities may be controversial, and students should seek advice before including them on a (e.g., pro-life or pro-choice abortion activities). Students may also want to avoid listing organizations that identify them by political party, religion, or ethnicity. On the other hand, many employers strive for diversity in their workforce, so this information could serve to positively differentiate a student.

Your child should avoid limiting his or her extracurricular involvement and employment to organizations which may seem one-dimensional or indicate a lack of ability to work with diverse populations. One student's included these entries: worked on a kibbutz in Israel, taught Hebrew at a synagogue school, and volunteered with B'nai B'rith. She later expressed regret that her lacked breadth. Another student majored in Afro-American studies, served as vice-president of the NAACP student chapter, chaired the publicity committee of the Black Cultural Center, and volunteered to tutor minority children. He developed good leadership skills but remarked that he wished his reflected his wide-ranging interests more effectively.

Employers sometimes ask questions to determine whether students have worked in organizations with members from different racial and cultural backgrounds. Regardless of your child's ethnicity, he or she should plan some involvement (campus activities, courses, or work experience) that demonstrates this exposure.

High School Burnout

Your child may decide as a freshman that he or she is burned out from student activities in high school, reasoning, "Since I have already proven my leadership ability to myself and others, why is it necessary to become so involved at college?" You may want to caution your child about the consequences of this approach.

Employers are likely to view high school accomplishments as ancient history. In fact, high school experiences do not usually belong on a college senior's résumé. Leadership roles in college present higher level challenges, since student officers may interact with faculty, alumni, senior campus administrators, and others.

What are some exceptions to the rule? A student who was editor of a prize-winning high school yearbook may want to include this achievement to her if it is relevant for an opening in the publishing industry, assuming she didn't use similar skills in college. School principals like to see that a prospective teacher has the background and interest to advise student groups, such as the yearbook or literary magazine staff, based on extracurricular activities in college or high school. (High school activities may be included on s of freshmen, sophomores, and juniors when applying for internships.)

Although extracurricular involvement is worthwhile, freshmen should begin with a modest time commitment. Their first priority should be establishing a good academic record.

The Double Agenda

Just as your child should take a strategic approach to choosing employment and campus activities, he or she should be forward-thinking with class assignments, so they also serve career goals. A professor may allow students to choose their own topic for an essay or speech. How can students tailor this type of assignment to their career interests?

A student who is interested in non-profit organizations that target social justice issues, may write an essay espousing abolition of capital punishment. An engineering major may write a paper analyzing the differences between civil and environmental engineering as a career path.

Students may also have discretion in choosing topics for an honors thesis or for an independent study project. For example, a student may decide to conduct a market research study of customer satisfaction in the banking industry. Employers are impressed when they learn that a student chose a subject that is relevant to a career interest.

Although many employers will consider students in any major for certain management trainee positions, an interviewer may wonder whether a history major, for example, is sincerely interested in business. Some recruiters are wary of applicants who appear to be just "shopping" or interviewing for practice. A student who has taken some business or economics electives and written a research paper on supply chain management, for example, may be a more credible candidate.

Some courses include an experiential component that helps students develop marketable skills. Business students are sometimes given a consulting assignment with a small business. They collect information about a specific problem and make recommendations to resolve it. Engineering and design majors at many universities are learning to apply their skills to social problems. They develop products that will benefit nonprofit organizations through social entrepreneurship programs. Students in certain psychology courses are required to perform related volunteer work. Alicia volunteered at a nursing home for three hours a week to satisfy a requirement for her "Psychology of Aging" class. As a result of her natural rapport with this population, she later targeted a job in gerontology and became the activities coordinator for a retirement center. ROTC students assume various positions of responsibility in the cadet corps and participate in a leadership lab.

National Competitions

Professional associations offer meetings, training, and conferences which students are usually welcome to attend. The annual Game Developers Conference is held in the California Bay Area, home of many employers which hire animators, special effects artists, engineers, and modelers. These companies also have openings in departments such as finance and marketing.

The Association for Computing Machinery offers an opportunity for students to demonstrate their skills and meet professionals through the ACM International Collegiate Programming Contest. In this IBM-sponsored event, prizes include $10,000 scholarships and computers or equipment for winning software programmers. Three-member teams include mathematics, physics, and computer science majors who work on computer games, chess, and applied mathematical problems. IBM has hired some winners to work in research and development positions.

Purdue University hosts the annual National Idea-to-Product (i2p) contest to solicit ideas to benefit nonprofit groups. Winners receive up to

$15,000 for costs of patenting their products. Another prominent program is the MIT $100,000 Entrepreneurial Competition, which must include one team member affiliated with MIT. Companies such as Boeing and Merck send employees to spot talented prospective hires. Students may compete in intercollegiate case competitions such as the Business Ethics Fortnight at Loyola Marymount University, sponsored in part by Northrop Grumman.

Government agencies also support contests for college students. The U.S. Environmental Protection Agency sponsors the P3 (People, Prosperity and Planet) Student Design Competition for Sustainability and the U.S. Department of Energy sponsors the North American Solar Challenge, a cross-country race with student-designed solar-powered cars.

Show and Tell

In some fields employers will ask students to provide a portfolio, writing sample, or other examples of their work. Advance planning will ensure that your child has appropriate samples to furnish. One employer reported that a student submitted a very personal diary entry as a writing sample! Here are some examples of career fields in which a portfolio may be necessary:

> **Consulting**-An employer may request a writing sample, usually a class assignment of at least three to five pages, as an example of research, writing, and analytic skills. Students should keep the best examples of their work.

> **Journalism**-Newspapers typically ask applicants to bring clippings to their job interviews. Examples could include articles written for a student newspaper, literary magazine, or other publication. A student can also apply to become a stringer for a local or national publication while in college, which will result in work samples as well as experience. Internships are another source of material, since student interns may write newsletter articles, press releases, and so on.

> **Art, Graphic Design, Advertising**-Employers in the arts or communications expect students to prepare a portfolio of their drawings, web pages, photography, or other work.

Technical Writing-Applicants in this field should collect samples of their work, such as instruction manuals, user guides, or articles about technical subjects. Ideal sources include assignments for a technical writing class or materials produced for an employer.

Broadcasting and Film-Employers in the media often request students to provide tapes of their work. Students may have obtained these tapes from experience with a student radio or television station, an internship, or a part-time job. In addition, students may make a tape specifically for consideration by prospective employers.

Some education majors have also begun to prepare teaching portfolios, some of them online, for prospective employers. These portfolios may include a student's sample syllabus or lesson plan, a videotape of student teaching, and pictures of bulletin boards or field trips.

Admissions officials from medical schools and graduate departments such as psychology report that they consider a student's research projects to be a plus, especially when supervised by a faculty member for publication.

Developing Relationships

College seniors are often stumped when asked to provide references on a job application or graduate school admission form. Students realize too late that they have not established close enough contacts with faculty members and other professionals. Since faint praise is almost as bad as a negative reference, students should be confident of a strong recommendation before requesting one.

It may not be easy for students to develop a relationship with professors at a large university, particularly during their freshman or sophomore year. How can a faculty member get to know individual students in an auditorium-sized classroom? A student can enroll in several classes that are taught by the same professor. In addition, a student can participate actively in class discussions and visit the professor during posted office hours to clarify difficult lecture points. Some students work for faculty as graders or research assistants. For students who take the initiative, faculty may become mentors and can be valuable sources of professional contacts for internships and job leads.

Academic advisors and other college administrators may be important contacts. They may oversee a club or other organization in which your son or daughter is active. These professionals may be in the best position to describe your child's leadership skills in a reference letter.

Faculty and administrators are also frequently asked to nominate students for special awards, honoraries, and fellowships.

Making Contacts

In addition to meeting career-related contacts through internships and informational interviews, students should identify and join professional associations in their field. Many of these associations charter student chapters on campuses, including Alpha Chi Sigma (professional chemistry fraternity), American Advertising Federation, American Chemical Society, and the Society of Professional Journalists.

As stressed in Chapter 3, eligible students should join academic honoraries of their major. Professionals sometimes interact with these student groups and may be a source of career information, internships and job leads. Some of these groups sponsor scholarships for members.

Students may also want to join a pre-professional club on their campus, such as the Pre-Law Club or Pre-Vet Club. These clubs usually invite guest speakers, such as graduate school admissions officers or professionals who discuss their occupations.

The college alumni association and the student affiliate group also can help your student make valuable contacts. These groups may arrange externships for students and offer other opportunities for them to meet alumni.

Some professionals make presentations in the classroom, participate in special events (such as a symposium or lecture series), and attend career fairs or panels on college campuses. Assertive students increase their visibility by asking good questions, helping to coordinate these activities, or following up later with a thank-you letter.

Student Contributions toward College Expenses

Many employers ask students how they financed their college education in order to determine the student's work ethic and sense of responsibility. "How many hours a week did you work during the school year?" "How many hours a week did you work during the summer?" "What percentage of your college expenses did you personally furnish?" "How much did you provide through work, loans, and scholarships?"

Some employers are favorably impressed with students who contribute a high proportion of their college expenses; however, students who work long hours (more than 20 hours per week) are less likely to have high grades, related experience (particularly internships), and leadership positions in campus organizations. If students have pressing financial needs, they should consider a combination of part-time work and loans in order to allow sufficient time for study *and* extracurricular activities.

Employers are often favorably impressed by honors such as merit-based financial awards, but a student with a full scholarship should still plan to obtain career-related experience.

Summary

Definition of an Internship

- A career-related experience that commonly lasts a semester, summer, or school year. It may be paid or unpaid, part-time or full-time.

Benefits of an Internship

- Exposure to a career field, industry, and employer

- Opportunity to develop and use marketable skills

- An advantage when applying for regular full time work

- A possible salary premium if offered a regular job with the same employer

- Contacts that may be useful for a job search

- References that are stronger and more relevant

- Development of job search skills before senior year

- Useful career experience (from both paid and unpaid internships)

Definition of an Externship

- A "job-shadowing" experience to observe a professional from half-a-day to a week

Benefits of an Externship

- Observation of activities may help a student determine whether to pursue a career.

- Contacts that may lead to part-time, internship, or regular job leads

Benefits of Self-Employment

- Development of skills and self-confidence

- Evidence of initiative, perseverance, and resourcefulness

Benefits of Extracurricular Activities

- Development of leadership, teamwork, and other skills

- Increased visibility with employers, through club programs and competitions.

- Mentoring, internships, employment, scholarships, and training opportunities gained through student chapters of professional associations.

Portfolios of Student Work

- Work samples requested by employers in some fields

Benefits of Relationships with Faculty and Administrators

- Identification of mentors
- Possiblefuture references

Benefits of Alumni Club and Professional Association Contacts

- Visibility to professionals in targeted career field

Conversation Starters for Parents and Students

1. What types of internships are available for someone in your field?

2. Which campus clubs or activities are you interested in? Which organizations, committees and offices are related to your career interests?

3. What are some ways you could develop samples of your work to show prospective employers?

4. Which of your faculty or administrators do you think might be able to serve as references for internships (or full-time jobs later)? How will you develop a relationship with them?

Resources

··

Tech-Interns.com
www.tech-interns.com (science and engineering)

Career Explorer
www.careerexplorer.net/internships.asp

CoolWorks: www.coolworks.com/internships/

InternWeb: www.internweb.com

WetFeet: www.internshipprograms.com

Transitions Abroad
www.transitionsabroad.com (Internships in Europe)

Intern Abroad Program: www.internabroad.com

Students.gov.
www.students.gov (federal government internships)

Global Experiences: www.globalexperiences.com

Virtual Internships: www.volunteermatch.org
www.serviceleader.org
www.internweb.com/virtual.asp.

CHAPTER 6

"I THINK I'LL GO TO GRAD SCHOOL"

....

One Ivy League law student was talking to his career advisor about his uncertain goals. Puzzled, she asked, "Why do you want to go to law school?"

His response was, "Because I didn't want to go to medical school." He wanted to go into a prestigious profession, and, since he didn't enjoy or excel in science, law seemed to be the natural choice !

....

Many students plan to continue their education for the wrong reasons. Help your son or daughter examine his or her motivation to attend graduate or professional school. Urge caution if you see these signs:

Lack of Focus - Is your child uncertain about a career direction and hoping to find it in graduate school? He or she may be still without focus two years (and $90,000) later. This is an expensive route to self-discovery and one that does not always work!

Pressure from Others - Does it seem that all of your child's friends are continuing their education? Some students find it difficult to be objective about decision-making when others–peers, family members, or faculty–offer their advice. Be sure your child seeks counsel from knowledgeable sources.

Misconceptions about the Job Market - Some students make the assumption that they cannot get too much education. They believe that a bachelor's degree is devalued today, "as common as a high school diploma used to be". Another misconception is that graduate training guarantees a higher starting salary. Recipients of some graduate and professional degrees do earn high incomes. However, those with a master's in social work, education, divinity, and many liberal arts fields actually earn *less* than many bachelor's degree recipients.

Immaturity - Few students look forward to the job search process. They are often anxious and fear rejection. Some students delay the inevitable by taking refuge in graduate or professional school.

Unrealistic expectations about graduate school - Further education is not simply more of the same undergraduate experience. Graduate students do not have much time for football games, parties, and other social activities, as they face 60-to 80-hour weeks of study and research.

Career Goal As Starting Point

Felicia, a second-year graduate student in speech communication, made an appointment to see her college counselor. "I've decided that I want to change direction. Human resources sounds interesting. How do I qualify for those positions?"

Ironically, a bachelor's graduate with related internships and courses may be more marketable to employers than someone with an unrelated master's degree. If an organization wants to recruit graduate-level human resources candidates, it would most likely target students with an M.S. in human resources or an MBA with a concentration in personnel management. Also, Felicia faces the likely interview question, "Why did you study speech communication if you want to work in human resources?"

A young person who starts with a career focus first and researches its educational requirements is less likely to enroll in a graduate program that is not necessary for her field or that will award an inappropriate degree. (Of course, some students may choose to continue their education for the sheer joy of learning without regard to the marketability of their advanced degree.)

Professional schools, such as those in law, medicine, and business, provide practical career training, while graduate degrees such as a Ph.D. or master's tend to be more academic in nature, emphasizing research skills. (See Table 6.1 for examples of graduate degree programs, their duration, projected job growth for degree recipients, and average starting salaries.)

Graduate school advisers wryly comment that, "In graduate school you learn more and more about less and less." One Ph.D. student was asked about his area of research. He responded, "Medieval Italian organ music."

Because graduate study is so specialized, students need to carefully select a career direction prior to enrolling. Is an advanced degree necessary to enter the field? Is a master's or doctoral degree recommended for advancement? If so, do employers prefer applicants who also have full-time work experience?

Choosing a graduate school is difficult if a student is not focused. Your daughter may excel in science and want to help people. She could apply to M.D. programs. Other alternatives include a master of science in genetic counseling, or a master's in neuroscience or public health. Among his many options are an M.A. in teaching English as a second language, museum education, and education administration.

Some new graduate degrees have been developed in response to world events, such as a master's degree in homeland security and in peace operations. Reflecting the trend toward multidisciplinary occupations, graduate degrees may be earned in fields such as medical statistics, biophysics, and biomedical engineering.

Graduate School Advisers

Most colleges and universities offer graduate school advising services. If your child is considering graduate or professional school, encourage him or her to consult an advisor as early as possible, ideally by the sophomore year.

Many health professions advisers have prepared lists of specific courses recommended for students interested in medicine, dentistry, veterinary medicine, and other programs. Medical school advisers strongly encourage students to take the MCAT in the spring of their junior year. Your child may want to request that admissions test scores be sent to his or her undergraduate adviser for use in the counseling process.

Here are some questions for your son or daughter to ask an adviser:

- Which prerequisites are necessary for graduate school admission?

- Which additional courses do you recommend to improve my chances of acceptance?

- Which extracurricular activities will help me develop relevant skills and be evaluated positively by admissions officers?

- Which work-related or volunteer experiences would enhance my credentials?

- Have alumni been especially successful at applying to particular graduate schools? Which schools?

- What qualifications do I need to be competitive?

- Do you have a timeline to suggest for the application process? For example, when should I register to take the graduate admissions test?

Researching and Evaluating Schools

You probably have a certain sense of deja vu as you watch your child consider graduate or professional schools. Didn't you do this just recently with regard to researching and visiting four-year colleges? Your child will weigh factors such as reputation of faculty, selectivity, cost, availability of financial aid, and location. He or she should apply to some schools which seem *too* selective for his credentials ("reach" schools), others that are a close match, and several that are "safe."

The stakes are higher as your child evaluates the quality of an institution's graduate education. Is the program accredited by the American Assembly of Collegiate Schools of Business (MBA schools), the American Bar Association (law schools), the American Psychological Association (doctoral programs in psychology), or whichever organization might be relevant?

Table 6-1

GRADUATE AND PROFESSIONAL SCHOOLS (EXAMPLES)

DEGREE	LENGTH STUDY	JOB GROWTH	STARTING COMPENSATION
Doctor of Jurisprudence (JD) Law	3 years	Average	Law firms: depends on reputation of school, class rank, size ($67,500 in small and $125,000 in large firms). State or local prosecutors and defenders): $43,000-$45,000
Doctor of Medicine (MD)	4 years plus residency	Faster than average	$200,000 (varies by specialty)
Master of Business Administration (MBA)	1-2 years	Faster than average	$88,591 (differs by quality of school and years of experience)
Master of Social Work (MSW)	2 years	Faster than average	$39,000
Doctor of Dental Surgery Dentistry (DDS)	3-4 years	Average	Less than 5 years in private practice: $149,350 (generalist) $315,160 (specialist)
Doctor of Pharmacy (PharmD)	2 years	Faster than average	$98,828
Doctor of Philosophy (PhD) Humanities, social sciences, liberal arts	4-8 years	Varies by discipline.	Assistant professor: $25,820–$47,390 (Highest paid: business, computer science, law.)
Natural sciences, computer science		Faster than average in computer, physical and some life sciences	$36,996 for first post-doctoral position; $78,000 for life science PhD and completion of post-doctoral positions
Doctor of Veterinary Medicine (DVM)	4 years	Average	Private practice: $71,000 (small animal) $60,000 (large animal)

Sources: National Association for Law Placement; Association of American Medical Colleges; Graduate Management Admission Council; American Association for the Advancement of Science; National Association of Social Workers; American Veterinary Association; American Dental Association, Survey Center, Survey of Dental Practice; American Association of University Professors

Some online resources allow your child to identify graduate or professional programs to consider based on certain criteria:

WEBSITE	SEARCH CRITERIA
www.petersons.com	Program, degree, location
www.topgraduate.com	Country, subject, and degree
www.princetonreview.com	Depends on degree program
www.gradview.com	Subject, location, public or private, size, country, degree

A student who graduates from one of the 193 law schools approved by the American Bar Association (ABA) may take the bar exam in any state. This privilege is not extended to graduates of the 41 non-ABA-approved or regionally accredited schools. Not all MBA schools are accredited by the AACSB, a distinction which may be noted by prospective employers.

Another consideration is the percentage of a school's graduates who pass professional examinations such as the bar (law) or boards (medical fields). A national comparison of 2006 bar exam results of alumni from non-accredited and accredited law schools revealed pass rates of 28 percent and 71 percent respectively. Your child should ask, too, about the number of students who obtain related summer internships or employment following graduation.

A student who has a strong geographic preference for employment may have an advantage by attending a business or law school in the same state or region.

It is possible that your child will be accepted by a mediocre graduate or professional school that is willing to take his or her tuition money despite a poor academic record. Graduates from undistinguished programs, however, often do not fare well in a competitive job market—even with the added degree.

Attending a foreign graduate or professional school is an option to consider; however, students may have difficulty obtaining employment in the United States after completion of their studies. Recipients of medical degrees from foreign or offshore programs tend to have a lower pass rate on the national licensure exam and generally are not selected for the most desirable residency programs.

Your child should consult faculty members and professionals in his or her field for advice about the reputation of graduate degree programs in other countries.

Joint Degree Programs

Some universities offer students the opportunity to graduate with two degrees simultaneously, such as law (J.D.) and MBA. These dual degrees generally require additional time. Students often ask college advisers about joint degree programs. Unfortunately, probing sometimes reveals that these students are unfocused about their career goals. They are interested in attending graduate school: law, business, history, something! By enrolling in a combined program they hope to increase their chances of getting it right. They assume that an additional degree will automatically give them a competitive edge, which isn't necessarily true. The increase in joint and dual degree programs has occurred in response to *student* demand–not *employer* demand. "Doing the Dual" is an article which provides an admissions officer's point of view on this topic (www.law-school-admissions.com/dualdegree.php). Combined-degree programs are a good choice for students who have a specialized or interdisciplinary career goal.

Most physician-scientists obtain an M.D. and a Ph.D. in a biomedical laboratory science, such as cell biology, genetics, and neuroscience. Graduates with an M.D.-Ph.D., offered by 120+ medical schools, may receive priority consideration for research-oriented residencies. Becoming a research physician requires up to 13 years of postgraduate training: 7-8 years pursuing an M.D.-Ph.D., a 3-year residency, and a 3-4 year postdoctoral fellowship. Students typically apply to these programs following their junior year in college. In addition to superior grades and MCAT scores, successful applicants are likely to have worked for a year (or several summers) doing research in the same laboratory.

Another attractive credential for M.D.'s is the MBA degree, a combination offered by 48 educational institutions. Executive search firms report that physician-MBA's are in demand as executives to run hospitals and HMO's. They also enter fields such as international health care consulting, technical licensing, and healthcare industry mergers and acquisitions. An M.D. with an M.S. in electrical engineering may perform product development for a medical device company. "Renaissance doctors" receive a combined degree almost unheard of a decade ago: medicine and the social sciences or humanities. Their interdisciplinary training focuses on issues such as global health or health research and policy.

Students interested in joint degrees need to identify universities with dual degree programs and determine their application process. In some cases students must apply separately to each program (e.g., business and law schools), and be accepted or rejected independently by each admissions office. Some M.D./Ph.D. in bioscience programs have a joint admissions committee. Your child should ask the career services staff of the graduate or professional schools in which they are interested about the types and number of employers requesting students with dual enrollment. An applicant may also want to inquire about typical starting positions and salaries for graduates of joint programs.

Enrollment in a combined program will usually shorten the time required to complete two degrees separately, but extend the time to complete one. For example, an MBA and J.D. can be earned in four years instead of five for each separately. (However, an MBA alone takes two years, and a J.D. alone takes three.)

Professional Schools

Medical School

Due to a projected shortage of physicians, the American Association of Medical Schools (AAMC) has announced a plan to increase enrollment by 30 percent in the next ten years.

The AAMC website describes what medical school admissions officers believe to be the high achieving student's dream job on its website (www.aamc.org/students/considering/careers.htm):

- **Opportunity to serve:** Allows you to help people.
- **Action:** Doesn't tie you to a desk all the time.
- **Respect:** You are an important part of your community.
- **Security:** Allows you a good living with a secure future.
- **Excitement:** Changes daily, so it's hardly ever boring.
- **Mobility:** You're in demand wherever you choose to live.
- **Flexibility:** Gives you lots of career options from the same education base.

The conclusion of the AAMC is that "Few occupations meet all of these standards. None meets them better than a career in medicine." After a downturn in applications during the years of transition to managed care, medical school has returned to its previous popularity among students.

Although superior grades and MCAT scores are important, medical schools also screen for personal traits and related experience. Successful applicants often demonstrate an early motivation for service through volunteer work in a health or community setting: for example, they began volunteering as college freshmen or sophomores with hospital patients, battered women, or abused children.

Can you imagine your child devoting five to eleven years to postbaccalaureate medical education? How will he or she fare during a residency of 24-hour days and 80-hour work weeks? Will your child remain composed and think clearly in the face of life-or-death decisions about a patient's treatment? Medical school admissions officers look for signs of applicants' compassion, intensity, self-direction, and ability to make quick decisions under the pressure of emergency conditions. Some applicants have undertaken an honors thesis requiring intense, focused, independent effort, or have performed volunteer work with a rescue squad.

Medical school advisers recommend that students take the Medical School Aptitute Test (MCAT) in the spring of their junior year or, at the latest, fall of their senior year. Pre-med students may choose any undergraduate major as long as they complete necessary prerequisites: generally two years of chemistry, one year each of biology and physics (with labs), and one year of calculus. (Requirements vary by medical school.) Your child should obtain a broad education in the sciences and liberal arts to be an attractive medical school candidate and to provide other options if not admitted

Your son or daughter may have difficulty choosing a career direction and only decide by senior year (or later) to become a physician. Postbaccalaureate pre-med programs are available at 82 universities (services.aamc.org/postbac) for graduates who lack prerequisites for medical school; however, this route often extends the time to achieve an M.D. by two to three years. It is more common than in the past for bachelor's degree recipients to obtain experience before applying to medical school. Some first join the Peace Corps, Doctors Without Borders, or Teach for America, while others may undertake fellowships or work for government health agencies.

Before completing applications your son or daughter should identify the institutions that are a match with his or her credentials and interests. The most selective schools accept less than three percent of their applicants; the overall acceptance rate is about 50 percent. Medical schools require personal interviews as the final step in the admissions process.

The cost of medical school tuition in 2007 for four years is about $122,000 at public medical schools and $158,000 at private ones. Average physican debt (including undergraduate loans) is $120,000, usually financed over a 20-25 year period. (Some lenders allow a 30 year payment plan!) If physicians want to join a practice or establish their own, they typically increase their indebtedness by $100,000-$300,000. Some admissions interviews include the question, "How do you plan to pay for medical school?" However, the return on investment can be worth it. During the first year after training, the most heavily recruited specialists are cardiologists, at an average annual salary of $320,000.

Choosing specialties that offer more work-life balance rather than the highest income, many medical students are attracted to fields such as dermatology, ophthalmology, and radiology. Opportunities for new physicians are more diverse than in the past, with options available in consulting, health policy, public health, and the military.

According to graduate school advisers, many pre-med students feel family pressure to enter medical school. Doctors, however, mention frustration with the increasing cost of medical malpractice insurance and lack of autonomy under managed care Your child should conduct information interviews with physicians to determine the advantages and disadvantages of entering the medical profession.

Business School

What are the new trends in MBA schools? Rather than requiring core courses in business functions such as marketing, finance and operations, many programs have created a new paradigm. Stanford University, for example, describes its MBA degree as "highly customized" for each student. After the first quarter, courses are offered at various levels of difficulty based on a student's background. Class content and a choice of 100 electives may be targeted to an individual's career objectives. Each student obtains international business exposure through an internship, exchange program, study abroad, or service-learning.

The University of Pennsylvania's Wharton MBA School refers to its program as "general management plus," which students obtain through the curriculum's breadth and depth. The School offers 18 majors and more than 200 electives. "Learning ventures" can take students to Quantico,

Virginia for exposure to U.S. Marine Corps leadership training. They can also choose Ecuador Mountaineering or an Antarctica Expedition, among other adventures.

Northeastern University's MBA students participate in a six-month paid "corporate residency" and M.S. in Accounting/MBA students obtain experience through a three-month co-op experience. International students may improve their English skills to score better on the TOEFL test and become more competitive for admission into a graduate business school through the Pre-MBA Program or Intensive English Program.

The Garvin School of International Management, also known as "Thunderbird," has consistently been ranked first among MBA schools with programs in global management. According to the Thunderbird website (www.thunderbird.edu), students use "Winterims," the period between trimesters, "to learn in the ancient hutongs in Beijing, the rainforests of Costa Rica, the Swiss Alps and the concrete canyons of Wall Street". Although students in most of its programs have an average of five years of work experience, recent college graduates may apply to for admission to Thunderbird's new one-year Master of Arts in Global Affairs and Management.

An MBA is a particularly good background for those who aspire to senior level management responsiblities or to entrepreneurship. Some career fields, such as brand management, are difficult to enter without an MBA. In addition, an MBA may be necessary to advance within some fields, such as investment banking and consulting. About half of MBA school entrants intend to change careers.

Highly-ranked MBA programs usually accept applicants who have at least three or four years of substantive full-time work experience. Applications to MBA schools fell during the last few years, resulting in the enrollment of less experienced students. According to The *Wall Street Journal*, MBA recipients in 2005 with at least six years of experience made an average salary of $70,516 before admission and $97,736 after graduation. In contrast, new MBAs with less than three years of experience earned an average of $40,606 before entering business school and $68,231 after earning the business degree.

Experienced students are more marketable in their job search, as employers seek those with related experience. As one MBA student observed, "All of us graduate with the same degree from the same school. What differentiates us is our background before entering the program."

Admissions officers strive to select a diverse student body. A typical entering class may include students who have been employed by large corporations, investment banks, consulting firms, non-profits, the military, small import-export firms, and hospitals.

The cost of an MBA degree from a top school can reach $150,000 in tuition, fees, and living expenses. Starting compensation after obtaining an MBA from a top-ranked program may be as high as $100,000-$165,000, including signing bonus (a one-time payment received upon acceptance of the job offer).

An undergraduate business major is not required to attend business school, although undergraduate business students may be eligible to enter an accelerated or joint BS/MBA program and graduate in less time. Many schools actually prefer other majors. For example, only 18 percent of recent MBA students at Stanford University were undergraduate business majors. Since most MBA programs are heavily quantitative, students should consider taking some undergraduate courses in areas such as calculus, accounting, statistics, operations research, and economics to prepare for graduate business education. Many schools offer pre-MBA courses on campus in the summer or online for new first-year students who need to sharpen their quantitative or computer skills.

Among accredited universities offering an online MBA are Duke, Babson College, and Thunderbird. Duke University's online program includes employees from organizations such as IBM, JP Morgan Chase, Proctor & Gamble, and the U.S. Army. Babson College's Fast-Track MBA combines Internet-based and on-site instruction (at Portland, Oregon or Boston, Massachusetts). Thunderbird students may choose the online Global MBA On-Demand Program, which requires one week each in Geneva, Switzerland and Beijing, China.

Law School

Does your child have keen writing and analytical skills? A logical mind? The ability to think quickly and not be fazed by confrontation? Is he or she thorough and detail oriented? Law could be just the right field. Recruitment at law schools has increased since 2005, resulting in many more offers for summer associate and regular job opportunities.

Many students choose a law career without doing adequate research on the profession. It seems like the default position for undecided students. Even students with a long-standing interest in the field sometimes find that law school is not at all what they had expected. The curriculum may seem tedious and formulaic as students learn to "think like a lawyer". Media portrayals of lawyers who work on high-profile trials or serve as advocates for worthwhile causes or groups are often appealing. The daily experience of most lawyers is much different, though: legal research and preparation of legal documents can be painstaking and routine. Your child should conduct information interviews with lawyers and seek summer or part-time positions that provide exposure to the legal environment.

The bar exam pass rate has dropped by 28% since 1995, leaving about 28,000 law school graduates each year with heavy debt and lost–or postponed–opportunity. The pass rate varies by state, from 62 percent in California to 90 percent in Utah in 2006. In some lower-ranked law schools, bar exam pass rates are 30-40 percent. Approximately one in four of those who fail the test do not re-take it. One disappointed test taker wrote online that he had failed the test for the fourth time and was applying for jobs as a law clerk, paralegal, legal assistant, and policy analyst. Another confided that he would spend a summer studying to take the exam again, "Oh, this is such a bitter pill that I have to swallow…"

If a law student discovers that his or her career choice was a mistake, it can be a costly one.

....

"I recently graduated from law school, and in the process have accumulated over $150k in student loans. I have quickly discovered that the legal path is not for me, and would like to attend veterinary school. I have no savings and no outside support, but have good credit. Is there any way I am going to be able to finance a veterinary education?"

Inquiry sent to vetmedicine.about.com

....

Pre-law students may choose any college major. If your child aspires to become a lawyer, he or she should develop excellent writing, research, analytic, and public speaking skills through course selection, extracurricular activities, and volunteer or work experience. The debate team, student government or honor court, and mediation training are all helpful experiences.

Law schools are starting to value full-time work experience more than in the past. About three-fourths of law students admitted by Northwestern University have at least two years of work experience, with only 6 percent accepted after receiving their bachelor's degree. A student may write a more compelling application essay and have an advantage obtaining employment in a targeted field with relevant experience such as nonprofit, government, or investment banking.

Law school curricula have traditionally emphasized legal theory and litigation rather than transactional (business or corporate) law. However, the majority of attorneys work in transactional law, expected by their firms to spend at least 2,000 billable hours a year protecting client interests through ironclad contracts, leases, and other documents.

Many law schools provide clinical education in which students gain practical experience representing clients in court cases under a lawyer's supervision or in moot courts (simulation cases). For example, Michigan State University offers opportunities for students to apply their law skills through its public-service externship program and law clinics related to rental housing, taxation, small business/nonprofits, and childhood advocacy. Some law schools offer certificate programs, concentrations, and study abroad options, which your child may want to consider to determine which school is most suitable.

Emory Law School and Georgia Tech have collaborated to offer a multidisciplinary program titled TI:GER (Technological Innovation: Generating Economic Results), which allows students to blend their knowledge of law, economics, management, science, and engineering in entrepreneurship.

More American lawyers are working in their firm's foreign offices or are dealing with international issues. As a result, law schools are recruiting applicants with foreign language skills and study abroad experience. Graduates with Chinese or Japanese language skills are very marketable. World events have led to elective courses on new topics such as war crimes, Islamic law, and immigration. Cyberlaw is an evolving field. Scientists with a J.D. are quite marketable in patent law for the U.S. Patent and Trademark office or in industry (especially biotechnology or information technology) interacting with inventors.

The acceptance rate at the most elite law schools is as low as 7.8 percent of applicants. According to the National Association for Law Placement, new graduates of the top ten schools, who join large law firms in major cities, earn the highest starting salaries, an average of $135,000. Most J.D. recipients begin their career with a small or midsize firm with fewer than 35 attorneys and salaries in the forties to sixties. Compensation also differs greatly according to the type of law practiced, with jobs in public interest or advocacy work paying about $40,000. The median salary for entry-level local and state prosecutors is $43,915 and $46,374 respectively; for public defenders it is $43,300.

Graduates of lower ranked law schools may have difficulty passing the bar exam, finding employment and be offered lower salaries. Some law school graduates enter alternative careers, such as mediator, arbitrator, FBI agent, legal researcher, politician, or lobbyist.

Law can be a prestigious and lucrative career choice, with the opportunity to share in the profits as partner in a law firm. However, large law firms promote only about one in eight lawyers to partner within seven to nine years and the others leave under an "up or out" policy. As a result, "law is one of the few fields where young professionals become less marketable as they get more experience," according to a *Wall Street Journal* article. Establishing a solo practice can be difficult, as it takes time to develop clients.

Veterinary School

A person with science ability, manual dexterity, ability to comfort animals and establish rapport with their owners, and composure in emergency situations may want to consider a career in veterinary medicine. Doctors of veterinary medicine (D.V.M.s or V.M.D.s) complete four years at a college of veterinary medicine. Veterinarians may become certified in areas such as dermatology, surgery, and dentistry after three years of additional education.

Opportunities for veterinarians exist in private practice, research, food safety inspection, and education. Demand is expected to be high for those in 20 veterinary specialties, such as toxicology, and immunology. The need is projected to be greatest in public practice areas, such as biosecurity and homeland security. A shortage of 1,500 public health veterinarians is projected to reach a shortfall of 15,000 in two decades.

If your child is interested in veterinary medicine, he or she should take courses in biology, chemistry, physics, and calculus. Experience working with a variety of large and small animals in settings such as a veterinarian's office, zoo, or animal shelter is desirable.

Since most veterinary colleges are public institutions, they tend to favor in-state residents. The acceptance rate to veterinary school is 43 percent, even more competitive than selection to medical school (www.avmc.org).

The average starting salary in 2006 for veterinarians in private practice was about $55,031; potential income for experienced veterinarians may exceed $118,000 a year. The average debt incurred during veterinary school is $100,805.

Pharmacy School

The annual salary increases of pharmacists grew faster in the last decade than any other occupation, according to Mercer Human Resources Consulting. Pharmacists now are required to obtain six years of education (which includes the B.S.) and receive a Pharm.D.; specialists need a total of eight years of higher education.

New pharmacy school graduates are receiving multiple job offers, a salary averaging $92,000, and a hiring bonus of up to $5,000-$20,000. The average salary for a retail store's pharmacy team manager is $104,300, and compensation for a regional pharmacy operations manager is $122,100. Most pharmacists work for chains such as CVS, Eckerd, and Walgreens. Others work for HMO's, government, hospitals, and pharmaceutical companies. The estimated shortage of pharmacists by 2020 is 157,000, according to the Pharmacy Manpower Project.

Dental School

If your child has science aptitude, manual dexterity, and good spatial perception and communication skills, he or she may want to explore dentistry as a career. Undergraduate course work for pre-dental students should include biology, chemistry, and physics. Applicants should try to obtain health-related experience, such as work in a dentist's office. Dental school requires four years of study after the bachelor's degree, and graduates receive the doctor of dental surgery (D.D.S.) or doctor of dental medicine (D.M.D.) degree.

About 80 percent of dentists are general practitioners and the other 20 percent specialize in areas such as orthodontia, pediatric dentistry, or periodontics (treatment of gum disease). Specialization requires two to four years of additional education following dental school.

Cumulative educational debt after receiving the DDS in 2005 was $104,483 at public universities and $161,500 at private ones. Median net income for self-employed dentists in 2004 was $185,940, with specialists earning as much as $315,160. Dentists have recently begun earning higher incomes with shorter work weeks than primary care physicians. Not affected as much by managed care or malpractice lawsuits, dentists are more able to control their costs and hours.

Pre-dental post-baccalaureate programs are offered at schools such as Nova Southeastern University, Creighton University, Tufts University, and Southern Illinois University. Admitted students must be state residents or from disadvantaged or culturally diverse backgrounds at some schools.

Social Work

Is your child interested in helping others and able to be compassionate and objective while dealing with others' difficult problems? Social work may be a career field to consider. A master's of social work (M.S.W.) is a marketable degree, and employment opportunities for graduates are projected to increase faster than average. Whereas a Ph.D. is required for licensure as a psychologist, the M.S.W. is a terminal degree that qualifies a social worker for many counseling positions.

Social work is a broad field, including practice in medical social work, school social work, employee assistance programs, child welfare and family services, gerontological services, mental health, and corrections. A social worker may establish a private practice, work as a caseworker or supervisor in a non-profit or government agency, teach, or conduct research. The mean salary for social workers is $51,192.

At some universities students with a bachelors in social work may be able to complete an M.S.W. in less time than the two years it normally requires. Students with other majors interested in social work should take undergraduate course work in social sciences such as psychology, sociology, political science, and economics. Social services experience, whether paid or volunteer work, is recommended before students apply to graduate school in social work.

Graduate School

··

Doctoral Degrees

Is your child passionately interested in his or her major? Would you characterize your child as high in creativity and academic and problem-solving skills? Has he or she demonstrated the ability to take initiative and be self-directed by carrying out a research project such as an honor's thesis or independent study? Does your child have the perseverance and intensity to complete a lengthy period of training that averages six years or more? Is he or she interested in college teaching and research? If so, graduate school in his or her chosen field may be the right option.

The Ph.D. (doctor of philosophy) degree provides students with broad knowledge in their field (such as political science, biology, or English) and trains them to do independent research to discover new knowledge. Graduate students spend the first several years taking classes, culminated by comprehensive written and/or oral examinations, or both. Next, they conduct research on a topic approved by a faculty committee. Students interested in pursuing a Ph.D. might want to think in advance about possible research interests.

Students should consult faculty members for recommendations of well-regarded graduate schools in their discipline. What are the areas of research for which each of the schools is known? Which faculty members at those institutions may be suitable mentors, based on their specialties and publications?

Many Ph.D. programs require proficiency in one or more foreign languages, such as German for psychology students and Greek and Latin for classics students. Graduate schools often prefer at least a 3.4 GPA in an applicant's major. Students with lower grades may want to enroll first in a master's degree program to prove that they are capable of graduate-level work.

Even if an applicant meets all the minimum criteria for acceptance (such as prerequisites, GPA, admissions test scores), competition is keen. Clinical psychology Ph.D. programs accept an average of 11-15 percent of applicants. Fifty to sixty percent of doctoral students do not complete their degree, reports the Council of Graduate Schools. For those who do obtain a doctorate, competition for jobs is fierce. As many as 300 applicants vie for each job opening in fields such as the humanities. It is common for Ph.D. graduates to begin their career in one-year appointments or part-time positions. Among Ph.D. recipients in 2004, about 30 percent were unemployed or planning to continue their studies.

Science Ph.D. graduates interested in academic jobs often need to work as "post-doc's," apprentice scientists at a university, before obtaining a position that can lead to tenure. The typical starting pay for a Ph.D. in post-doc laboratory jobs is $36,996 for new graduates. In some cases they do not receive benefits, as they are neither students nor regular employees. Research universities employ far fewer Ph.D.'s in science and engineering than in the past.

....

During orientation to a Ph.D. program in the life sciences, incoming students were told that they would need to spend approximately six years obtaining their degree and five or more years doing a postdoc assignment.

One student exclaimed, "Do you mean I'll be in my early thirties before I get a real job?"

The faculty member responded, "If you are lucky."

....

Ph.D.'s in business, nursing, speech pathology, and veterinary medicine, among others, are needed to fill faculty vacancies. Graduates with relevant doctoral degrees are also being eagerly sought by consulting firms, government agencies, and pharmaceutical companies where they may find a more stable and sometimes less stressful environment. They no longer have to worry about obtaining funding for research, publishing in the right journals, and teaching courses to students with varying degrees of motivation.

Starting salaries vary widely by field for doctorate recipients, even for jobs at the same institution. An assistant professor in business may earn much more than a faculty member of the same rank in psychology. Faculty members with doctorates in engineering, computer science, health and physical science tend to be paid more than those in fields such as the liberal arts. The percentage of assistant professors achieving tenure at the same institution is about 55-60 percent. Ph.D. graduates in all fields typically receive higher salaries outside colleges and universities.

Master's Degrees

A master's degree is less time-consuming, less expensive, and less intensive than a doctorate and is sufficient preparation to qualify for many career fields. A master's in education is generally necessary for school counselors or college student personnel professionals and a master's in library or information science is required for most library jobs. Archivist or curator positions require a master's degree.

A master's in social work is necessary for many social services positions. Geriatric care managers qualify for their positions with a bachelors in nursing or gerontology and a masters in social work. Those with a master's degree in social science or public health are qualified for positions in social or behavioral research. Urban and regional planners with a masters in public administration are more competitive for government jobs than bachelors graduates.

Applicants in several health occupations, like public health, hospital administration, and physical therapy, find these fields easier to enter with a master's degree. For speech language pathologists and audiologists, a master's degree is required. Students with a master's degree in chemistry, computer science, operations research, and statistics are marketable for many positions in industry.

The Alfred P. Sloan Foundation has worked with the private sector to develop two-year professional science master's degrees at 45 colleges and universities. These degrees are typically multidisciplinary and emphasize applied science and mathematics over theoretical study. They are offered in fields such as applied computing, bioinformatics, environmental science and assessment, forensic chemistry, geographical information systems, health physics, human-computer interaction, prosthetics and orthotics, and zoo and aquarium science management.

According to the Sloan Foundation, about 70 percent of the content of professional science-related master's degrees is science-related and 30 percent the same as in MBA schools, such as project management, negotiation, manufacturing, and product development.

A master's degree in a liberal arts field, such as English or history, is the minimum qualification to teach at a community college. However, Ph.D. candidates also apply for these positions and are considered more qualified. A master's degree in these fields may not necessarily increase a student's marketability for positions in business or industry.

Application Costs

The expenses of applying to graduate or professional schools can add up quickly. Test preparation can cost $35 for a practice exam from the test service publisher, $100 for software from a bookstore, and up to $1400+ for 100 hours of instruction from a commercial test preparation service. The price of an admissions test ranges from $105 for the Pharmacy College Admission Test to $250 for the Graduate Management Admission Test. A university application fee can range from $35-90 each, and it's not uncommon for a student to apply to 10 schools. The cost of a centralized application processing service, which distributes test results and other materials to multiple schools, can be $200-450 for students who apply to the average number of law or medical schools.

Some graduate or professional schools require a personal interview, which involves travel expenses. After acceptance by a school, the deposit required to reserve a space may be around $600, which is typically nonrefundable if the applicant decides to attend another school.

Timing of Graduate Study

Even if your child is accepted into graduate or professional school, his or her plans may change. Many students suddenly decide during spring of their senior year to take time off from education before making a commitment to a demanding course of study. Other circumstances may alter or delay your child's graduate school plans, such as changes in family financial circumstances. A back-up plan is valuable in these situations.

Deferred enrollment is an option sometimes available to students. Graduate schools are often supportive of delayed matriculation, since they value students with additional maturity and certainty about their goals.

Many students say that they believe that graduate study is a "now-or-never" proposition. Once they become accustomed to a job with a steady income, they reason, it will be much more difficult to return to college. For some students that may be true.

However, there can be good reasons to delay graduate education. Not every college senior is certain about a career direction. Work experience may help a graduate clarify strengths, weaknesses, and interests. It may help in determining whether further education is necessary. Graduate school applicants often have more maturity and stronger qualifications as a result of working several years.

Some organizations offer generous tuition reimbursement plans for employees who take job-related courses part-time, which helps avoid heavy debt. Other employers may fund the entire cost of graduate study, sometimes allowing the employee to attend full-time with the stipulation that he will return to work for a specified length of time after graduation. For example, the military covers the cost of medical or law school for very strong applicants, who incur a military obligation upon graduation.

Some analysts at investment banks or consulting firms, described as "rare stars" by one employer, may be reimbursed their MBA school tuitions if they return after graduation. They commit to remain with the firm for at least three or four years.

What If Your Child Isn't Accepted?

Despite an intense desire to become a lawyer (veterinarian, dentist, psychologist, etc.) and impressive credentials, your son or daughter may not be accepted into graduate or professional school. Many students are ill-prepared to begin a job search when they receive rejection letters from graduate schools as late as April or May of their senior year. Attractive employers have often filled their openings through on-campus interviewing by February or March.

Encourage your child to prepare a backup plan as an alternative to graduate or professional school. What are some ways to do this? Even though your son is applying to law school, he could also interview for positions as a policy analyst, legal assistant, or campaign worker for a political candidate. If your daughter is applying to medical school, she could also interview for openings as a pharmaceutical sales representative, staff consultant for a firm specializing in the health care industry, or research technician at a hospital or university. As one medical school admissions officer put it, "People with backup plans are probably less likely to need them–they have prepared themselves with a broad perspective instead of doggedly pursuing one narrow goal." Students applying to extremely selective programs, such as clinical psychology, may want to apply to related professional school programs, such as counseling or educational psychology.

Students are often eternal optimists when it comes to their graduate school prospects. "I'll reapply next year," your son may reassure you following rejection by all five or ten schools to which he applied. Graduate school admissions officers say that students may obtain useful feedback by asking why they were turned down. Would it help next time around if your son took additional upper-level courses in his major? Perhaps related work experience would tip the scales in his favor. Some applicants are accepted to graduate school after reapplying. However, if nothing changes in the intervening year or so between applications, the result is likely to be the same.

It reflects positively on their maturity if they have used the intervening time productively. A medical school admissions officer, asked for examples of worthwhile activities during a year between applications, retorted, "Not lounging in Cancun or Ft. Lauderdale!" One student volunteered with Mother Theresa for a year in India and found medical school admission officers eager to interview her. Other examples of constructive experience include the Peace Corps, Teach for America, laboratory research work, and educational outreach programs for public health departments.

Applicants should show a willingness to move on with their lives instead of waiting indefinitely for acceptance; they should write a new essay when they reapply to reflect their activities and growth since their original application.

If placed on a waiting list, your son or daughter should follow up periodically with the admissions office. A wait-list student could be notified of acceptance as late as the day before classes begin if someone else drops out suddenly.

Special Programs

Some college graduates enroll in short-term educational programs designed to provide specific career-related skills. Examples are paralegal training, business and publishing institutes, and a design program.

Paralegal Schools

The paralegal field is one of the fastest growing occupations, according to the U.S. Department of Labor. Paralegals may conduct interviews with clients and witnesses, research records such as titles and deeds, draft wills and trusts, and perform many other duties to assist lawyers. According to the International Paralegal Management Association, the average 2006 compensation for paralegals was $58,496, including bonus and overtime. Paralegals who were corporate or environmental specialists made more than $100,000 in annual compensation.

Although students at some universities may obtain a bachelor's degree in paralegal studies, graduates with other majors can also acquire these skills through three-to six-month programs at paralegal schools. Formal paralegal education is not always necessary, as some employers hire new college graduates and provide them with on-the-job training for these positions.

For graduates who take time off before law school, a paralegal or legal assistant position may be an ideal temporary, transitional job. They have an opportunity to observe the legal profession in practice and can more realistically decide whether or not to attend law school.

Publishing Institutes

Students who enjoyed working on a high school or college publication and who have strong skills in writing, photography, graphic arts, marketing, or public relations may benefit from attending a publishing institute.

Publishing institutes typically last four to six weeks and cost $4,700-$6,600. The Columbia Publishing Course in New York City offers six weeks of "total immersion." The four-week University of Denver Publishing Institute provides graduate-level studies on book publishing topics, such as editing and marketing. Students who complete the New York University Publishing Institute may acquire credits toward an M.S. in Publishing. More information about these and other programs may be obtained at www.bookjobscom (see "about publishing" and "publishing programs/education").

Business Institutes

Non-business majors may want to consider a special summer institute to acquire basic business skills before beginning their job search. These programs last three to six weeks and cost from about $4,000-8,500. Examples of some business institutes are Babson Business Edge, Babson College; Business for Arts Sciences, and Engineering (BASE) Summer Program, University of California at Berkeley; Carolina Business Institute, University of North Carolina at Chapel Hill; Tuck Business Bridge Program, Dartmouth College; and McIntire Business Institute, University of Virginia.

Additional "business bootcamp" programs are offered by George Washington University, New York University, Southern Methodist University, Stanford University, and Vanderbilt University. Business institutes typically introduce students to basic principles of accounting, finance, business statistics, management, and marketing. They also provide seminars for students on job search skills and opportunities to meet employers. Attendance before a student's senior year is advantageous so that he or she may list the courses on a résumé and discuss them during interviews.

Introduction to Design Careers

Harvard University's Graduate School of Design offers a six-week summer program, "Career Discovery," to introduce high school graduates, college students, college graduates, and professionals to careers in architecture, landscape architecture, urban planning, and and urban design. Participants gain exposure to the design field and are able to evaluate whether they have the interest and potential to pursue a related degree. This intense program includes lectures, studio work, career counseling, and field trips.

One-Year Graduate Programs

Bachelor's graduates of any major can obtain professional credentials in 12-15 month master's degree programs in fields such as accounting or school counseling.

The Massachusetts Institute of Technology offers a nine-month master's in engineering, targeted at engineering bachelor's degree recipients who are interested in application-oriented course work rather than research. Students may choose among three tracks: Environmental and Water Quality Engineering, High Performance Structure, and Geotechnical.

Graduates with a bachelor's in education and an A-level teaching certificate may earn a master's in special education or early childhood education at some institutions in one year. College graduates without an education major can study for a Master of Arts in Teaching (MAT) and teaching licensure.

Certification Programs

Non-education majors may qualify for a teaching certificate by taking two or three terms of course work. Even without this background, students in majors such as mathematics, physical sciences, and foreign languages are often hired by school systems because of critical shortage of certified teachers in these areas. Some states require non-education majors to pursue teacher certification through "lateral entry" programs. They enroll in education courses during evenings or summers.

College graduates may prepare for other employment options through enrollment in certificate programs. Northeastern University offers an extensive list of subjects (www.spcs.neu.edu/postbac), such as instructional design, knowledge management, digital media, clinical trial design and project management, bioinformatics essentials, game design, marketing technologies, and intellectual property.

Health careers may be entered with one-year post-baccalaureate certificates in fields such as medical records administration or cytotechnology.

Summary

....

Reasons to Attend Graduate or Professional School

- An advanced degree may be required to enter a desired career field

- An advanced degree may make a job applicant more marketable and result in higher compensation

- Sheer joy of learning

Reasons Not to Attend Graduate School

- Lack of a career focus

- Pressure from friends or family

- Misconceptions about the job market

- Lack of maturity

- Unrealistic expectations about graduate school

What to Do When Considering Graduate School

- Determine career goals first

- Meet with graduate and professional school advisers

- Research course prerequisites, optimum timing for admissions tests, helpful extracurricular activities, and other preparation

- Consider cost of degree and financial resources

- Have a back-up plan

Typical Admission Application Components

- Personal essay or statement, written in an interesting, narrative style

- Letters of recommendations

- Graduate admissions test (test preparation is necessary)

- Transcript

Conversation Starters for Parents and Students

1. Why do you want to go to graduate/professional school?

2. What kind of qualifications do you need to be competitive for graduate study?

3. Which faculty members or advisers do you think would be good references? What do you think each would say about you?

4. Have you considered doing research or independent study?

5. What preparation will you need to do your best on the admissions test?

6. Do you want to take time off before graduate school? What would you do?

7. Have you considered a back-up plan to graduate school?

8. How many schools do you plan to apply to? What expenses do you expect to incur in the application process? Have you thought about how to finance graduate study?

Resources

....

General Information

QS: The world's leading network for top careers and education: www.qunetwork.com

Grad school search (country, subject, degree) www.topgraduate.com

Princeton Review: www.princetonreview.com

Business School

Graduate Management Admissions Council: www.mba.com

Business School Admission: www.businessschooladmission.com/

All Business Schools: www.allbusinessschools.com

Law School

Law School Admission Council: www.lsac.org/

Dental School

Student Doctor Network: www.studentdoctor.net/dental/

American Dental Education Association: www.adea.org

American Dental Association: www.ada.org

Medical School

American Association of Medical Schools: www.aamc.org

Medical School Admissions : www.medicalschooladmission.com

On The Road to Medical Science: itsa.ucsf.edu/~jcholfin/toc.html

Veterinary School

American Association of Veterinary Medical Colleges
www.aavmc.org/

Combined Programs

www.bestpremed.com/MD-PHD.php

services.aamc.org/currdir/section3/start.cfm

International Students

*TOEFL iBT with CD-ROM,*2005: Simon and Schuster

CHAPTER 7

TAKING TIME OFF AFTER COLLEGE

....

A university career services office sent an email message to a recent graduate, who had not yet found a job. An automated email was returned with the following message:

"I may not have access to my email until March because of my stay at a Buddhist meditation center in West Virginia."

....

The transition from college graduation to first job is not what it used to be. If you went to college, some of your graduating classmates may have taken the summer off to travel before buckling down to an earnest job search. Perhaps a proud and generous grandparent funded a grandchild's trip to Europe. In other cases, new graduates celebrated their independence by backpacking through a foreign country on $10 a day with the help of a dog-eared paperback guide.

The conversation among today's college seniors is quite different: "Should I teach English in Japan, track wildlife for a research project in Tanzania, or learn to take underwater pictures with The Great White Shark Project in South Africa?"

Taking a "gap year" before or after college has been a long-time tradition for students from affluent families in the UK. American college graduates started "taking time off" in increasing numbers in the 1990's.

Some may feel burned out after four or five years of college and want a break before entering graduate school. Others say, "I don't want a 'real job' yet." What *do* they want? "Oh, something fun and different - not an 8-to-5 desk job," as one student explained. Friends from earlier graduating classes provide advice for college seniors: "Travel now while you can, before you get tied down by a job with only two weeks of vacation or a family and mortgage."

Testing possible career choices or building skills to become more marketable motivates some students to plan a time off experience. Still others need to do some soul-searching to clarify their values. How will they identify their "calling" or niche in the world? (Parents who are baby boomers may be able to reflect on their own quest to "find themselves".)

Students have many reasons for wanting to take time off after graduation (see checklist below). Discussing these with your child can help identify the types of experiences that will be the best fit.

Some students also consider taking time off during college, such as . However, this may require them to drop out of college, re-apply for admission, and lose health insurance during their absence. It is important for your child to check on university policies regarding these matters.

Here are some examples of time off pursuits that appeal to many new graduates:

Travel, study or work abroad

- Teaching English in a foreign country

- Volunteer work such as Peace Corps

- International travel/ study programs

- Independent travel

- Training for a sports competition

Domestic volunteer work or internship

- Working for a non-profit agency such as Teach for America

- Volunteering for a religious organization

- Working for political campaign, member of Congress, or lobbying or social activist group

Temporary or contract work

- Working for a variety of industries, companies, and departments

REASONS FOR TAKING TIME OFF

Students: Check your reasons for wanting to "take time off":

☐ 1. I'm not sure what I want to do and need time to explore possibilities and make decisions.

☐ 2. I feel burned out and don't have the energy to begin a demanding career or graduate degree.

☐ 3. I want to work, travel and/or study abroad

☐ 4. I want to study further, volunteer or work at a short-term position to develop additional skills and confidence before conducting a job search.

☐ 5. I want to work in a fun job (dude ranch, cruise ship, resort, etc.) before settling down to a more traditional, career-oriented position.

☐ 6. I want to be geographically close to someone special before committing to a career or graduate school, which may require a separation.

☐ 7. I want to make a meaningful contribution through public service, religious, or volunteer work.

☐ 8. I want to test out a possible career field before making a commitment (e.g. work as a legal assistant before entering law school).

☐ 9. I want to do something adventurous that I may not have another opportunity to experience (Outward Bound, etc.)

☐ 10. I want to gain exposure to many industries, career fields, and prospective employers.

☐ 11 I want time to study fitness for life-long benefits (tai chi, yoga, pilates), to train for an athletic competition, or become a certified instructor in a sport.

☐ 12. I want time for spiritual growth or to live a more simplified life.

Check responses with Answer Key on page 175.

Adventure or hospitality industry jobs

- Working for a dude ranch, resort, or cruise ship

Two-year analyst or other short-term programs

- Working as an analyst for an investment bank or consulting firm

- Working as a legal assistant for a law firm

Parents may be skeptical about the value of options that delay career employment or graduate school enrollment. You may wonder how this experience will be evaluated by prospective employers or admissions officers and question whether your child's interest in time off is a sign of an inability to make a commitment or accept responsibility.

Time-off experiences are so different that it is difficult to generalize about their value. Working as a waiter, whether in Paris or in Colorado Springs, is not likely to be regarded as advantageous by most employers seeking college graduates. Volunteering their time in tsunami and Hurricane Katrina recovery efforts may be viewed differently.

Advantages and Disadvantages

Advantages

There are several advantages to taking time off: Your child could become more certain about a career direction through temporary, volunteer, or other short-term work. With additional perspective, maturity, and experience, your child may avoid a poor fit in that first "real" job.

An interim period may give a graduate who truly is burned out a chance to "recharge batteries" so he or she is able to approach a real job or graduate school with energy and commitment. Some alumni express regrets about **not** having taken the opportunity to travel or perform extended volunteer work before they assumed financial, job, or family commitments.

For future careers with a global focus, such as international business or international development, there is no substitute for living and working abroad for enhancing cross-cultural and language skills. Post-graduation may be the optimal time to obtain this experience before other commitments make it more difficult. Some graduates develop or enhance skills and obtain valuable experiences that increase their marketablity for future employment or credentials for graduate school admission. Your child may also gain additional maturity, adaptability, and polish as a result of foreign travel.

For many non-profit jobs and admission to professional school programs, volunteer work is especially beneficial. Students may also earn educational benefits from some volunteer organizations that will assist with the cost of future graduate study.

Disadvantages

Although there may be valid reasons to take time-off, some employers evaluate this negatively. They may assume that this applicant:

- does not have a strong work ethic and is not eager to begin a real job.

- lacks maturity and places more importance on travel, leisure time, or "self-discovery" than on employment, or is content to be supported by his or her parents indefinitely.

- lacks job-related skills. (Employers may not recognize marketable skills in nontraditional settings such as dude ranches. A graduate may have to be persuasive to convey the valuable elements of hospitality or service jobs, such as public contact, customer service, and teamwork.)

- has been unable to find a job.

Major employers often structure management training programs to coincide with college graduation schedules. Training programs generally begin in June or August, with job offers extended to applicants as early as the preceding January. Some new graduates take several months off to travel and return home ready to start a job search. The result can be many missed opportunities. (Some employers, such as J.P. Morgan and Bain, allow students to defer their starting date of employment while working for

Peace Corps or Teach for America. Students may even be allowed to keep their signing bonus.)

Employers consider it legitimate to ask why an applicant has delayed the job search. So your son or daughter should be prepared to answer the question, "What have you been doing since graduation?" Spending all summer at a beach or ski resort sounds far less impressive than working for a temporary service while preparing to relocate with a spouse.

When asked about time-off experiences, one recruiter noted that "Grades and college activities fade in importance with time." What is an employer's first impression of John's résumé during his senior year at college? He is an honors student and senior class president. One or two years later, he is identified just as quickly by his occupation: a waiter at a resort.

Working at a low-paying job or borrowing to finance a structured "gap year" experience following graduation may leave recent degree recipients in debt or without funds to re-pay college loans. The cost of short-term gratification has left some young adults with poor credit histories that take years to overcome.

Some graduates find that a job in a glamorous location is hard to leave after a summer or a year. Consider it from their perspective: They enjoy an environment with beaches, mountains, or a desert and a ready social life with other recent graduates. The prospect of searching for a real job seems distinctly unappealing.

Each time-off experience should be considered on its own merits. This chapter provides an overview of possible options.

International Options

Many students want to acquire or enhance foreign language skills, particularly if they aspire to jobs in international business, foreign affairs, or other work requiring fluency in a foreign language. They may also want to travel, experience a different culture, or volunteer to help make a difference in a developing country. Some possibilities for obtaining international experience are teaching English in a foreign country, study-abroad programs, internships, volunteer work, language study programs, and independent travel.

Evaluating International Experiences

Your daughter wants to go to Japan to teach English—or to a Yugoslavian work camp to restore historical monuments—or to wait tables in London. Her excitement is almost contagious. "This is the chance of a lifetime," she says. "I will get to travel and gain international experience, and it will help me get a job later." But you have concerns. Not too long ago you worried how she would adjust to life 200 miles away at State University. Now she wants to go thousands of miles away!

Each day you think of another concern: Will she be safe? What if she has a medical emergency? Where will she live? How much will it *really* cost? Will this experience be just a pleasant detour, unrelated to her future goals and throwing her off track? Here are some questions to ask your daughter about travel abroad, particularly if she will be affiliated with a structured program.

Organization sponsorship--What do you know about the sponsoring organization, its source of funding, and reputation? Is it affiliated with another agency? Are its goals consistent with your values?

Health and safety--If health insurance is provided, what does it cover? Is local health care adequate? Which immunizations do you need?

Training and orientation--What kind of training or orientation is provided for program participants? (It may be critical to learn about local laws or customs. For example, some countries' laws have *severe* penalties for drug use or public consumption of alcohol.)

Housing--How difficult is it to find housing? Are there options such as homestays (renting a room from a local family) or university housing?

Living and working conditions--How does the environment differ from what you are used to? If it is described as "spartan," exactly what does that mean? Will you be isolated or part of a group? Will you be the only American in the group? If the entire group is American, will the experience provide you the exposure you want

161

to other cultures? Will the program include other participants your age?

Costs and income--What are transportation and other program expenses (e.g. application fee, room and board, insurance, and tuition)? Are you eligible for a salary, stipend, or deferment or cancellation of student loans during this period? Is financial assistance available?

Foreign language skills--Are your language skills adequate? Will you receive sufficient language training through the program?

Marketability and relationship to career goals--Have you checked into how prospective employers or graduate schools evaluate this type of experience? Does the organization offer an "alumni" group that provides networking opportunities? Will this opportunity confer advantages for future employment, such as with the federal government? Is there another program that would open more opportunities?

Visa status--What type of visa do you need, and how difficult is it to obtain? (Some graduates plan to work on a tourist visa, although it is illegal to do so.) What is the duration of the visa or work permit you will be issued?

Support services--How much support will the program provide if you have problems? For example, what if the housing or internship is not what you were promised, or political instability or illness make it necessary for you to leave earlier than planned? Some organizations promise job leads, which may turn out to be little more than classified ads.

Developing Countries: A Special Note--Living abroad may sound romantic to your child, but the reality may be jarring for those who go to developing countries inEastern Europe, Southeast Asia, Latin America, and Africa.

Is your child really prepared to live without electricity, hot water, heat, and air conditioning? What are the health risks? Your child should contact the Centers for Disease Control before traveling to foreign countries to determine which immunizations are advised and should check the U.S. State Department website to see if the country he or she plans to visit is on the "Do Not Travel" advisory list.

Teaching English Abroad

Surprisingly, some positions teaching English abroad require neither previous teaching experience nor foreign language skills; however, returning teachers strongly recommend that applicants first obtain teaching or tutoring experience to qualify for more desirable assignments and to enhance their effectiveness on the job.

What kind of background have previous graduates found helpful? Some of them have served as a teaching assistant for a professor or tutor for other students. Others have volunteered as an English conversation partner for international students, taught English as a second language to immigrants, or tutored adults through a literacy program.

Your son or daughter may want to enroll in a two to four week course for teaching English as a foreign language at a local college or in the destination country. CELTA (www.cambridge.esol.org), Trinity College (www.trinitycollege.co.uk), and the Language Academy (TLA) are highly regarded and offer a TESOL (Teacher of English to Speakers of Other Languages) Certificate, which increases marketability for students who aspire to teach English abroad. Many employers are more likely to pay for roundtrip airfare and make a job offer to an applicant prior to relocation if he or she holds this qualification. Schools in foreign countries that offer a certification program sometimes provide their graduates with employment assistance or contacts for potential employment.

Information on job market demand, compensation, and working conditions for English teachers in various countries can be found at www.english-international.com/.

According to this resource, a student who has a parent or grandparent with citizenship in a European Union country will have an advantage in teaching English in Western Europe.

World Teach is an organization that hires college graduates to teach primary (grades 1-6), high school, university, or adult students for a summer or a year in developing countries. The cost to students for service in the Marshall Islands or Pohnpei State (Micronesia), for example, is $1,000, which is refunded at the conclusion of a one-year commitment.

The Japanese Exchange and Teaching Program (JET) matches college students with jobs in Japan. The program guarantees a comfortable salary, and sponsoring employers (boards of education, government agencies, etc.) pay for round trip air fare from designated U.S. locations. JET provides its teachers with extensive training, including orientation during pre-departure from the U.S. and after arrival in Japan. Participants are encouraged to learn Japanese during their stay in the country. Students must make a one-year commitment, which is renewable for up to two years.

Princeton-in-Asia (webscript.princeton.edu), a non-profit agency associated with Princeton University, places teaching fellows abroad in 14 Asian countries. A smaller number of PiA fellowships are offered in the fields of journalism, international development, and business. Living conditions and salaries vary by location, which may be urban or rural. The program is not limited to Princeton students or alumni.

Your child should thoroughly research a potential teaching assignment. One graduate applied to teach English in China and accepted an assignment without consulting a map. The result? He arrived in Harbin, China and was shocked to find himself on the edge of Siberia.

Is your child self-reliant, enthusiastic, flexible, and creative? Teaching English in a foreign country can be a "sink or swim" endeavor. As one former teacher put it, "Don't expect any hand-holding!" Some alumni have expressed dismay at the very traditional attitude of Japanese society towards women.

What jobs do former teachers take after finishing their commitment? Those in Japan sometimes remain in the country to apply for other opportunities as translators, writers, or editors. International banks are sometimes interested in college graduates with international experience and foreign language skills for positions working with global or emerging markets.

Some former teachers look for work in non-profits or government agencies. One worked as a recruiter for the Peace Corps after serving with that organization in South America. Another worked at the State Department for the United States Agency for International Development as a contractor for the Europe and New Independent States Bureau on urban development and housing projects. The only technical program assistant without a masters degree, she was confident that her experience in Slovakia made the difference.

International Volunteer Work

Work Camps

Eric participated in a workcamp in Lefkada, Greece during the summer after his junior year in college building roads with other volunteers ages 19-35. Reflecting on the experience, Eric remarked that, "It was hard physical labor–I can identify with prisoners on chain gangs!"

Work camps, small groups of volunteers from various countries, are sponsored by organizations such as Volunteers for Peace (wwwvjp.org), and Church of the Brethren (www.brethen.org). The American Friends Service Committee (www.afsc.org), a Quaker ministry, sponsors a Mexico Summer Project and China and African Summer Workcamps.

Participation in Volunteers For Peace requires $20 for registration and a $250 fee for most of the 2-3 week international service trips. (Roundtrip travel to the location is paid for by volunteers.) The work varies and can include constructing low income housing, providing social services, and helping with historic preservation or archaeology projects. The website is frank about this type of experience: "If you are only interested in tourism or a cheap vacation, do not register for this program."

Peace Corps

The Peace Corps (www.peacecorps.gov) sends nearly 8,000 volunteers to serve two-year assignments in 70+ countries in the Caribbean, Latin America, Eastern Europe and Central Asia, North Africa and Middle East, Asia, Africa, and the Pacific Islands. The median age for volunteers is 25; 96% have earned at least a bachelor's degree, and 13% have done graduate work. An excerpt from a Peace Corps website illustrates the agency's openness to applicants from diverse backgrounds:

"Many applicants are concerned that their specific major or field of study does not match up directly to any Peace Corps program. Don't worry! Many Peace Corps volunteers are college graduates with degrees in liberal

arts such as history, political science, English, social studies, or psychology. Others have degrees in photography, theater, and other fine arts. And of course, people with degrees in business, engineering, and the sciences have skills that translate well to many Peace Corps programs, including business development, environmental programs, information technology, and health education."

....

The Peace Corps provides outstanding support services for volunteers. They receive three months of training, paid expenses, a living allowance, medical and dental coverage, and deferral or partial cancellation of certain educational loans. In the event of political instability, they are evacuated to safety. Volunteers also receive 24 vacation days per year and may invite family members to visit.

Following 27 months of training and service, volunteers receive additional benefits, including a $6075 "readjustment allowance," possible reduction of educational loans, career counseling, and non-competitive eligibility (preferential consideration) for federal jobs.

The Peace Corps has a website for Family and Friends that includes an "Interview with a Peace Corps Dad".

Religious Organizations

Students and graduates may study Hebrew and work on a kibbutz (www.kibbutzprogramcenter.org/) or travel to Israel for a "working holiday" through the Kibbutz Adventure Centre, which provides free room and board. Many religious organizations sponsor opportunities for college students and new graduates to serve in overseas missions. They may help build a new church, school or playground, give religious instruction to children, or teach English as a foreign language (www.kibbutz.com.au/).

Habitat for Humanity (www.habitat.org/) is a housing ministry that includes Global Village teams who participate on international short-term (9-14 day) house-building trips alongside future homeowners and local volunteers. Although the work requires hard physical labor, volunteers also have time to tour historic sites such as ancient ruins, museums and churches. Not including airfare, costs to volunteers range from $1,300-$2,200.

The Association of Camphill Communities in Great Britain (www.camphill.org.uk/) consists of communities in the United Kingdon with residents of all ages, many of whom have disabilities. Volunteers have their own room within this communal living arrangement, developing close relationships with others who eat and reside in the same building. The program lasts from six to twelve months. Volunteers receive training in the spiritual, psychological, social, and therapeutic components of the Camphill treatment philosophy and receive free room and board and a modest monthly allowance. Travel costs from another country are sometimes partially reimbursed upon completion of a commitment. (The organization also has locations in the U.S.)

Other Work Abroad Options

Transitions Abroad

Transitions Abroad (www.transitionsabroad.com) is a site that provides information for students with interests in international travel, study, living, and work, or allows them to combine these interests. From international internships to au pair, teaching English, and farm work, this organization offers a broad selection of programs. Your child can explore opportunities in 45 countries, Argentina to Venezuela, as the organization's website shares facts from the Association of American Residents Overseas (www.aaro.org) about "The Essential Expatriate Resources" such as housing, healthcare, visas, and work permits.

BUNAC

BUNAC (www.bunac.com) provides programs lasting from five weeks to two years for students to volunteer and teach abroad. Some of the locations include Ghana, South Africa, Cambodia, Costa Rica, Peru, Russia, and China. The volunteer experiences vary from conservation to education and social services. Students may also obtain Teaching English as a Foreign Language (TEFL) training online through BUNAC.

CIEE

The Council on International Exchange Service (www.ciee.org) offers opportunities for American students and graduates to study and teach abroad. It also helps international students obtain professional training or seasonal work in the U.S. CIEE provides insurance for students or recent graduates through its iNext card.

International Study

Language Schools

A graduate who wants to study a foreign language while immersed in another culture may consider attending a language school abroad. Courses typically last a minimum of one month, although some vary in length from two weeks to a semester or a year. Universities and private language schools offer language study programs.

Factors such as location, class size, student-teacher ratio, length, cost, methods of instruction, and hours of instruction should be evaluated. Some language schools use multiple teaching methods, including conversation groups, language tapes, tutors, and field trips. Daily instruction may last four to eight hours, with additional preparation time expected out of the classroom. Schools may offer homestays and access to non-language courses such as art, architecture, history, and geography.

Language proficiency requirements for applicants differ by school. Some accept students without any foreign language skills; others require prospective students to pass a proficiency test or provide a transcript showing four semesters of college-level language.

Specialized Study Programs

There is a study program for virtually every subject. If your child is interested in learning about art history and art-related careers, Sotheby's Education Studies (www.sothebysinstitutelondon.com) features lectures and tours of museums and the auction house by experts. The program helps students to find internships at a Sotheby's auction house or at galleries and art institutions where many alumni of the Institute work.

The Year Out Group (www.yearoutgroup.org/) consists of many organizations that satisfy diverse "time out" goals. Some examples include: Greenforce (environmental expeditions), Peak Leaders (ski and snowboard instructor courses), Tante Marie (cooking school), Frontier Conservation ("Dive. Teach. Trek. Explore."), The Leap Overseas (eco-tourism and conservation projects), and Year Out Drama.

Teaching and Projects Abroad (www.teaching-abroad.co.uk) places students in career-related volunteer settings, including medicine, journalism, business, and law.

Domestic Volunteer Work or Internships

New graduates sometimes volunteer or accept modest wages for environmental, social activist, or non-profit groups for a year or two. Examples of these programs follow.

Americorps, often dubbed the "domestic Peace Corps," recruits volunteers to assist communities for nine months to three years in education, public safety, human services and the environment. Volunteers receive a stipend during their service and an Americorps Education Award for $4,725 at the conclusion of their commitment. Part-time workers may be eligible for a partial award. Other benefits include health coverage and deferral of payment on student loans.

Lutheran Volunteer Corps (www.lutheranvolunteercorps.org) is a one-year volunteer service program in the U.S. for applicants who want to deepen their spirituality, simplify their lives, and work toward social justice. Volunteers work in one of nine inner city locations in fields such as education, public safety, the environment, and social services. Spanish is required for some placements. Some volunteers become salaried professionals at agencies where they worked.

The Jesuit Volunteer Corps (www.jesuitvolunteers.org) is dedicated to the philosophy that its members should combine the four values of "community, spirituality, social justice and simple lifestyle". The organization stresses that volunteers have the right motivation to serve: "Do not apply if your primary reasons are that you don't have any other plans, can't get a job, and want to improve your résumé."

Community Homestead (www.communityhomesteads.org) in rural Wisconsin features "lifesharing houses" where volunteers work with people who have special needs. A list of religious retreats is available at www.findthedivine.com.

Green Corps is a popular environmental lobbying group that recruits graduates interested in environmental issues. They learn to use lobbying techniques to increase citizen and legislator awareness of environmental problems. If participants work with Green Corps for 13 months, they receive a salary of $14,500 a year plus benefits. Americorps volunteers may work with the Neighborhood Green Corps for 10 months; they receive a monthly stipend and educational award after working on service projects in communities.

Teach for America recruits new college graduates to teach in inner-city and rural schools for two years. Designed for non-education majors, the program sends new teachers to an intensive six-week training program before they report to their assignments. They also receive support from a mentor teacher. Up to 60% of the recruits have remained in public education after completion of their obligation.

New graduates may be interested in volunteering or working at entry-level jobs for members of Congress, political parties, and lobbying or advocacy groups. Especially during a campaign year, many opportunities are available to assist political candidates at the federal, state, and local levels. Recent graduates help recruit volunteers, staff telephone banks, and assist with fundraising.

Temporary Or Contract Work

For a graduate unsure about a career direction but eager to try out a number of possiblities, temporary work may be beneficial. Where else can someone work for a publisher, university, accounting firm, and manufacturer within the same month?

Many employers are reluctant to take a risk on job applicants for full-time positions. Temporary and contract firms are a boon for employers who want to save recruiting, screening, and benefits costs while staffing short-term assignments.

There are a number of benefits to temporary work for college students or new graduates:

- Exposure to different industries, companies, and departments

- Potential to learn new skills on the job (including free training from temporary firms in skills which are in short supply)

- The opportunity to be considered for regular employment

- Additional experience to include on a résumé

- Contacts that may be useful for networking, job leads, and references

- Income during a job search, while becoming established in the arts (such as acting, painting, writing, or music), or supporting travel.

The first dilemma may be how to decide which temporary firm to contact. A graduate who wants to work for specific companies should call their human resources departments to ask which temporary firms they use. If your child is interested in a certain industry or functional area, he or she should identify the agencies that specialize in these areas. It *is* acceptable to register with several different agencies.

When your child applies to temporary firms, he or she should ask about assignments more likely to lead to permanent employment (temp-to-perm) or to develop marketable skills.

Whether the job is challenging or mundane, a temporary employee–like any other employee–should try to exceed the employer's expectations. Good work performance, a positive attitude, and initiative may lead to further assignments. Your child should be open about his or her job search. A temporary may be asked, "Are you new?" An example of a recommended response is: "I'm working as a temporary in the marketing department while I look for a job in pharmaceutical sales. I recently graduated from Simmons College with a biology major."

Your child should determine how temporary work fits in with a job search strategy. A series of short-term assignments may finance day-to-day expenses and allow time to schedule interviews. Some temps work three or four days a week or for several weeks with time between assignments.

Others take long-term projects of several months to learn new skills, make networking contacts, acquire references, and position themselves to hear about openings before positions are advertised.

Which candidate is more likely to penetrate the "hidden job market": the one who is paralyzed with inertia and sitting at home watching TV talk shows, or the one who works at CNN this week and IBM the next? Encourage your child to make the most of temporary work as he or she is finding the right niche.

Contract Firms

The contract firm often provides benefits for its employees, unlike many temporary firms. Contract firm work assignments tend to be longer in duration than those with temporary agencies. It is not unusual for contract employees to work for the same client for years at a time.

When one assignment ends, the contract employee remains on the payroll until placed with another client. Temporary employees risk intermittent periods of unemployment between assignments.

Adventure And Hospitality Jobs

Your son or daughter's vision of the ideal job after graduation may center less on the position than the place. Many students dream about jobs in exotic locales: tropical islands, mountains, beaches, ranches, or cruise ships. Employers of choice may include those in tourism and adventure companies: amusement and theme parks, ski resorts, tourist submarine companies, hot-air balloon companies, and tour excort companies.

What kinds of jobs are available for new graduates in these settings?

- **Resorts** hire front desk clerks, secretaries, accounting clerks, cooks, wait staff, gift shop clerks, lifeguards, bartenders, and bellhops. (**Ski resorts** in addition hire ski instructors, lift operators, and snowmaker operators.)

- **Amusement parks** hire singers, dancers, photographers, ride operators, animal handlers, tram operators, admission cashiers.

- **Adventure travel companies** hire tour guides, photography and video staff, and food service personnel. **Hot air balloon companies** hire balloon pilots, ground crew and "champagne celebration hostesses".

- **Ranches** hire wranglers, campfire entertainers, ranch cooks, and farm hands.

- **Cruises** hire assistant cruise directors, disk jockeys, sound and light technicians, youth counselors, magicians, vocalists, instrumentalists, and wait staff.

If your child accepts a minimum wage job with a wait staff at a ski resort, you may be quick to point out the disadvantages of low pay, undesirable hours, poor benefits, and lack of advancement opportunities. But after taking the job, what is she most likely to talk about? Skiing during her lunch hour. Despite your evaluation of this type of experience, your child may consider it the best time of his or her life.

It may surprise you how well your child can live on a hospitality job. One graduate reported that she made $80-130 a day in wages and tips at a ski resort restaurant. "People bring a lot of money on vacation. They're in a good mood, and they tip generously," she explained. "The job also offered special perks, such as discounted ski passes."

If your child is interested in resort, adventure, or tour escort jobs, certain skills could prove to be an advantage: CPR and Red Cross first aid certificates, bicycle repair skills, camping, tennis, skiiing, horseback riding, and photography.

Many resort jobs are seasonal, such as from Memorial Day to Labor Day. Others require a commitment of eight months to two years.

Employers in these fields may limit consideration to applicants who have already relocated and can interview in person. One finance graduate from Seattle University worked in sales for Cruiser Bob's Original Haleakala Downhill on the island of Maui, Hawaii. This unusual tour company leads bicycle trips down a volcano. Bob Kiger ("Cruiser Bob") only hires applicants who live on Maui. "Camping out on the beach" doesn't count, he notes; however, he says that it is not difficult to obtain employment in the service industry once an individual decides to move to Hawaii.

Some graduates may find their niche in the hospitality industry, which often promotes from within for management jobs. Hospitality employees who later apply for unrelated jobs may find themselves stereotyped by prospective employers. Waiting on tables or operating a cash register, no matter how glamorous the surroundings, may not be considered relevant background for jobs requiring a college degree.

Short-Term Business and Law-Related Options

Analyst Programs

Does your child want to work for a while before continuing his or her education? For a graduate with very competitive qualifications (high GPA, internships, leadership activities), a two-year analyst position may be perfect. Investment banks and consulting firms offer these opportunities, designed for exceptional students who want a demanding job without a long-term commitment. Analyst positions are especially desirable for those who are interested in future graduate business education. Some firms offer analysts job opportunities that do not require further education following the two-year program.

Analysts often enjoy the variety of working on projects that provide exposure to different departments, companies, industries, and regions. This breadth allows them greater perspective in evaluating future career decisions. Analysts receive advice from their predecessors who have successfully entered business school and from admissions officers.

Top-tier MBA schools actively recruit analysts for admission. These applicants typically have well-honed quantitative skills and broad exposure to problem solving for businesses in different industries.

Legal Assistant/Paralegal Work

Is your son or daughter considering a career as a lawyer? Some legal firms, district attorney's offices, and government agencies hire new bachelor's-level graduates for a year or more as legal assistants or paralegals. This provides them with exposure to the law profession and a break before beginning another three years of education.

White & Case (legalasst@whitecase.com), an international law firm based in New York, assigns legal assistant clerks to a practice specialty such as litigation or trust and estates. The firm asks applicants for at least a two-year commitment. The U.S. Department of Justice hires new graduates for a two-year Paralegal Program in its Antitrust Division.

REASONS FOR TAKING TIME OFF
(Answer Key to Page 157)

....

Responses 1, 4, 6, 8, 10
Consider work with a temporary service or contract firm to explore your career interests and types of employers. You may also apply for two-year analyst positions. Internships are another possibility for testing out possible career fields. If you are considering a law career, you may want to work as a legal assistant.

Responses 2, 5, 9
Several websites at the end of the chapter are helpful for identifying options in hospitality or adventure fields. Can you acquire skills related to your future career goals with an employer in the location you desire? For example, someone interested in public relations may apply for jobs in guest services, sales, and other related areas.

If you feel burned out, how long do you need to re-charge your batteries? Some employers will allow new graduates to take time off before starting work—from a few months for travel to two years for Peace Corps or Teach for America programs, so beware of passing up opportunities to interview during your senior year. You could graduate with a job *and* time off. Volunteer work may help you overcome burnout as you are helping others.

Responses 3, 7, 9
What kind of time commitment are you willing to make? (Some programs, such as teaching English abroad and the Peace Corps, require participants to commit to a one-or two-year period.) Do you need to earn a salary or a stipend to cover incidentals, or can you afford to pay for the experience? (You could make enough to save money while teaching English in Japan, whereas other options could require a fee up to several thousands of dollars.) Will you need to work for an agency whose volunteers qualify for deferral of college loans?

Response 6
Before you make decisions that involve sacrificing career or educational

opportunities, discuss the level of commitment you and your special friend have in your relationship. (One student was prepared to limit his willingness to relocate to remain close to a girlfriend, only to learn that she was not as serious about their relationship as he was.) If you decide to stay in a particular location, consider working for a temporary service or a national company with offices where you may be able to transfer in a later move.

Response 11
If you have strong interest in certain forms of fitness, you may want to devote time to serious study to incorporate them into your lifestyle. Maybe you want to become certified to teach a sport or train for an important competition.

Response 12
Before beginning a commitment to work or study, you may want to devote more time to your spiritual life through a retreat, pilgrimage, or conference. A mission trip or service project may also be an option. You may ask for guidance from your spiritual adviser. Faith-based organizations to consider include the Lutheran Volunteer Corps, Jesuit Volunteer Corps, Habitat for Humanity or Association of Camphill Communities.

Summary

....

Possible Reasons for Taking Time-Off:

- Uncertainty about career direction

- Burnout and lack of energy for a job search or graduate school

- Desire to gain skills or experience before a job search

- Opportunity to serve through volunteer work

- A chance to test out a variety of career fields

- Time to do something fun before taking a career position

- Time to train for athletic competition

- Desire to travel

Evaluation of Time Off by Employers and Graduate Schools

Positive

- Enhancement of an applicant's skills and experience

- An increase in career focus

- Demonstration of risk-taking, adaptability, planning, and taking responsibility for a project, sometimes involving teamwork with a diverse group

- Demonstration of a commitment to service (for non-profits, medical schools, etc.)

Negative

- Questionable maturity and motivation

- Lack of career-related experience (depending on how the time has been spent)

- Less recognition after time for honors

- Management training programs already filled when a graduate is ready to begin a job search

Typical Time-Off Options

- Travel, study, or work abroad

- Domestic volunteer work or internship

- Analyst programs (investment banks, consulting firms) and paralegal positions

- Adventure or hospitality industry jobs

- Nondegree study programs

- Temporary/contract work

Considerations Relating to Going Abroad

- Organization sponsorship and support services

- Health and safety; living and working conditions

- Training and orientation

- Costs, income,loan deferment or partial cancellation, financial assistance

- Marketability/relationship to career goals

- Visa status and duration

Conversation Starters For Parents And Students

....

1. What are your plans immediately after graduation?

2. Why are you considering taking time off? What professional and personal goals do you have for this period?

3. How do prospective employers or graduate schools evaluate the type of experience you are considering? Do you know anyone who has recently returned from this type of experience or program?

4. What length of time are you planning to commit to this experience?

5. How do you plan to finance this experience?

6. How will you arrange for health insurance?

Resources

∙∙

"Hopping off the School Track: Should You Take Some Time Off?"
(www.princetonreview.com)
"Volunteering to Explore Career Possibilities."
(www.serviceleader.org

"What is Taking Off?" (www.takingoff.net)

"Should You Take A Year Off After Graduation?"
(www.delayingtherealworld.com/)

Opportunities Abroad (www.goabroad.com/)

CHAPTER 8

BEGINNING THE JOB SEARCH

Your child's senior year will come faster than you can imagine. (Surely it was only five or six years ago that you were teaching her how to ride a two-wheeler!) But you have your bankbook to prove that your child has indeed made it through three (or more) years of college and will soon be graduating.

While you are beginning the year with much anticipation of being tuition-free (at least for this child), your child may be feeling great anxiety.

Graduating college students face a time of uncertainty unlike anything they have seen before. Not only are they unsure about what they will be doing next year, they do not know where they will be doing it, nor for whom. To make matters worse, they can't even be certain that they will find a job!

Students are aware of the competitive job market; they realize that it may be difficult to find work after graduation. They have heard the stories about the fraternity brother who graduated last year and is waiting tables or the young woman next door who spent months looking for a job and finally found one selling satellite dishes door-to-door (on straight commission).

The fear of failing can nearly paralyze students in their senior year. Students who haven't done early career planning often do not have confidence that they will succeed in the job market. They may avoid using the career office and may procrastinate about getting started on their job search until the last possible moment—perhaps only a few weeks before graduation.

We hope, though, your child has taken the advice of this book and has been preparing for a career throughout college. If so, there is every reason to believe that the job hunt will be successful, given a little realism, flexibility, and persistence.

The exercise at the end of this chapter ("Job-Hunter's Reality Check") may be useful for helping your child assess his or her qualifications. It can be a good tool for the two of you to discuss at the beginning of the senior year. (This exercise can also be helpful for a sophomore or junior, because it will indicate areas needing work.)

Where To Start

Where and when should students begin their job search?

If they have engaged in career planning as recommended, they have actually started their job search long before their senior year. Their exploration and decision making to determine their career choice; their participation in extracurricular activities, part-time jobs, and internships/co-op experiences; and their contacts made through networking, career fairs, and professional associations have put them in a strong position to now find a job. They are already far ahead of most seniors, many of whom are just beginning some of these activities.

We recommend that students actively begin job hunting at the beginning of their senior year. In fact, some ambitious students may want to update their résumé, compose cover letters, and begin researching employers during the summer after their junior year. Even students who are planning to apply to graduate or professional school would be wise to pursue employment as a backup plan, since many applicants are not admitted. (By the time such applicants learn this, however, it is typically late April—often too late to begin trying to take advantage of the many interviews and other job-related opportunities offered by their campus career office.) See the recommended timeline below for the senior who has done the preparatory career planning work.

Many books are available on the job search; in fact, there are entire books devoted to each of the job search steps, such as writing a résumé, interviewing, and networking. In this chapter, the *basics* of the job search are covered.

The Tools

1.   The Résumé
"Who am I anyway? Am I my résumé?"

So goes the line from the popular Broadway show *A Chorus Line.* To the graduating student, the answer is *yes.* Generally speaking, the job-hunter *is* his or her résumé, and vice-versa.

The résumé represents the job-hunter's qualifications to the prospective employer and should make a polished first impression. It is essential that the résumé be done well and represent the student in the best possible light.

The résumé is the most critical tool in determining whether job seekers will be granted an interview (unless the job seeker has a close contact with influence with the employer). It is the interview itself, rather than the résumé, that actually determines if the candidate will be offered the job.

At the end of this chapter is an outline of a recommended résumé format as well as the résumés of two students - one a technical major and one a liberal arts major.

Typically the sections on a college senior's résumé include:

- **Name and contact information**

- **Objective**

- **Special Skills (optional)**

- **Education**

- **Honors (optional)**

- **Relevant Coursework (optional)**

- **Leadership Activities (optional)**

- **Relevant Experience**

- **Other Experience**

- **College Activities**

- **References**

Below are important guidelines for the résumé of a graduating bachelors-level student:

1. Keep the résumé to one page unless you have had a number of significant work or leadership activities that require a second page.

2. Be absolutely sure that the résumé is error-free (no typos or misspelled words) and is easy to read. (Use adequate spacing and type size, and highlight categories with bold-face print. Do not underline anything.) In a poll of senior executives, the single most common mistake given on résumés of job-seekers was typos or grammatical errors.

3. Use good quality white or off-white bond paper.

4. Begin with name, address, e-mail address, and telephone number. Be certain that the email address is appropriate and professional. (As an example, the address mary_carter@school.edu is fine; southernsweetie@school.edu is not.) Two addresses (home and school) and telephone numbers (home and school or cell) may be listed. Fax number may be listed if available.

5. Do not include height, weight, date of birth, social security number, health, salary desired, or a photograph.

6. Do not include high school information unless you graduated from a prestigious private school (it is then acceptable to include the name of the school and date of graduation) or were awarded a significant honor, such as valedictorian.

7. Use an objective that is brief and to the point (e.g., "An entry-level position in market research," "A position in software development," "A position utilizing my communication and mathematical skills"). If a résumé will be on file with the career office for their use, the objective should be one that applies to all of your career interests or else should be eliminated.

8. On a résumé that will be used through the career office, include college GPA if it is above a 2.5; for use outside the career office, include the GPA if it is above a 3.0. Also include your GPA in your major if it is noticeably higher than your overall GPA (.2 or more) and if your major is relevant to your job objective.

9. If you are combining GPA's from different colleges attended, be sure to calculate the combined GPA correctly and to indicate clearly on your résumé what you have done.

10. If you have worked more than 20 hours during the school year to personally finance college expenses, indicate this on your résumé. This can help explain a modest GPA.

11. Include all academic and other honors, such as merit-based scholarships, Dean's List, honoraries, or achievements (in sports, music, and academic competitions or challenges). Briefly explain them if they are not self-explanatory, e.g., "Order of Omega" (leadership honor society).

12. List work and significant extracurricular experiences in reverse chronological order (most recent first). Begin with position title, followed by employer or organization, location (city and state), dates of employment or participation, and description of responsibilities and accomplishments. For less-significant extracurricular activities, simply list your role ("Member," "Secretary," etc.) and the name of the organization.

13. If you have two or more experiences relevant to your career goal, separate experience into sections entitled "Relevant Experience" and "Other Experience". Otherwise, use one section labeled "Experience." You may include entrepreneurial activity such as selling goods on e-bay, providing computer technical support, designing websites, etc. as experience. This shows initiative.

14. Use active verbs when describing work and extracurricular experiences. It is not necessary to describe less significant jobs such as lifeguard, bank teller, file clerk, unless you can describe how you excelled above others in the same position, the title does not adequately describe the work performed, or if these were your only jobs. Simply list these jobs with title, employer name, dates, and place of employment. However, if promoted to head lifeguard or server, you may want to indicate how many employees you supervised, as an indication of your leadership skills.

15. Do not minimize the importance of significant leadership roles in volunteer or campus organizations. Place these under "Relevant Experience" or "Leadership Experience" if appropriate.

16. Write the résumé in outline form, using short, staccato phrases, such as "Created publicity campaign for campus blood drive". Do not use pronouns (such as "I created...") or complete sentences.

17. Wherever possible specify results achieved and quantify responsibilities and results (e.g., "Raised over $10,000 for homeless shelter," "Ranked #1 among 12 salespersons for the summer," "Tutored ten students in upper-level Spanish").

18. Include special skills such as knowledge of computer languages or software and hardware, foreign languages and laboratory skills in a section entitled "Special Skills." If these are relevant to your career goal, place this section near the top of your résumé (after the Objective). Otherwise, place it near the bottom, above "References".

19. Other optional sections are "Community Activities," "Military Experience," "Publications," "Professional Associations," "Certifications," "Licensures," and "Interests and Activities".

20. Be cautious about listing activities that reveal religious and political affiliation or sexual orientation on your résumé unless all of your leadership experience is with these organizations or they are related to your career goal (e.g., you have worked on a political campaign and are now applying for a job on Capitol Hill). Some employers have prejudices.

21. References should be the last item on the résumé and should be handled with the statement "References Available Upon Request". If asked, be prepared to provide a separate list of three references, including name, title, address, telephone, and email address (usually two employers and one faculty or academic adviser/administrator, or vice versa).

22. Never put any information on your résumé that is not completely true.

23. Be careful about "rounding-up" your GPA; a 3.29 may be rounded to a 3.3, but a 3.26 should not be. When in doubt, play it safe and give the complete GPA (3.26) or check with your career office.

24. Do not use standardized templates to create your résumé unless it is one recommended by your career office.

Employers receive hundreds of résumés in the mail each day. A résumé must be perfectly done and have strong content in order to positively stand out.

Your son or daughter should draft a résumé and take it to the career office to be critiqued. He or she should not rely on a friend, a big brother (even if he wrote a résumé a few years ago which helped him land a job), an aunt, or you (even if you are the personnel director of a large company) to write his or her résumé.

All of these people can help with the first draft, but counselors in the career office are usually in the best position to know what most employers seek in the résumé of a new graduate. College career counselors have contact with hundreds of employers in a large variety of fields. If your child knows the personnel director of the XYX Company and wants to work for the XYZ Company, by all means, he should seek advice about his résumé (and other aspects of the job search) from this contact; however, keep in mind that this person is an expert on the *XYZ Company*, not necessarily *all* companies. Some organizations have preferences that are unique to them, and a student may be given advice that will not serve him well with other organizations.

Many large organizations such as the Ford Motor Company now require applicants to apply and complete a fairly lengthy questionnaire online in order to be considered for employment. The online application usually takes the place of a résumé and is specifically tailored to determine a match between the employer's needs and the candidate's qualifications.

2.   The Cover Letter

Writing a good cover letter is an important skill for anyone seeking a job. It is amazing how many well-educated job hunters do not know the correct format for a business letter! Below is an outline of the correct format.

Most employers today state that it is acceptable to send both the cover letter and résumé by email, although some recommend that it be followed up with a hard copy sent by mail. If sending by email, it is best to include the text of the cover letter in the actual body of the email as well as to send it as an attachment. The résumé should be sent as an attachment.

When mailing, the letter should be printed on good quality bond paper that matches the paper and font type and size used for the résumé, attached to the résumé by paper clip, and sent in a large brown envelope to avoid having a crease. Some résumé paper has large envelopes that match.

Whenever possible the cover letter should be written to a specific person (e.g., "Dear Ms. White"). A student who does not have a contact name should make some effort to obtain one: he or she might check with the career office, the campus alumni network, the organization website, directories, or even call the organization and ask for the name of the director of human resources (sales manager, etc.). If a name cannot be located or the student is responding to a post office box listed in a classified ad, the letter should be addressed, "Dear Sir or Madam".

A cover letter should typically be about three paragraphs long and limited to one page. The content should not repeat in detail the information on the enclosed résumé but rather should highlight the information on the résumé and in the student's background that significantly relates to this specific organization (and position, if known). The letter should also indicate *why the student is interested in this particular organization* and should present a strong case for *how the student might contribute to it.*

Job hunters often mistakenly approach the cover letter from the point of view of what the organization can do for *them.* Although this is, of course, their primary reason for writing, they must view the cover letter and résumé as a marketing tool and indicate what they have to offer the employer. (Would a salesperson try to tell you what he will gain if you buy his product?)

If the student has been referred to the employer by a particular person (perhaps Uncle Jack, who is a vice president of the organization, or the director of the career office), the student should mention this at the beginning of the letter. Employers, like most of us, tend to pay more attention to a referral from someone they know.

Although most job-hunters will draft a basic cover letter, it must be individualized for each employer so that it reads as if it were written specifically for that organization. The organization's name should appear in the letter (e.g., "I am very eager to work for Nike," rather than, "I am very eager to work for your organization"), and the letter should contain several sentences indicating that the writer has researched the organization and knows something about it.

Students should close their letter by stating that they are eager to talk with the employer and that may be reached at _____phone number and email address. They may also state that they will contact the employer to follow up. This approach is more impressive than the typical passive one of asking to be contacted if the employer has interest. It also enables the student to get some quick feedback from the employer since it does not put the student in the position of waiting for the employer's response - which may never come!

Students should have one or two of their cover letters reviewed by a career counselor before sending them. Even if confident about their writing skills, students sometimes have trouble getting a business-like tone. Obviously there should be no grammatical or spelling errors.

COVER LETTER FORMAT

22-A Summit Place
Los Angeles, CA 90049
October 10, 20xx

Ms. Judith Martinez
Director of Marketing
Cameron Manufacturing, Inc.
1500 Main Street
St. Louis, MO 63124

Dear Ms. Martinez:

(*Opening paragraph*) State why you are writing, name the position or type of work for which you are applying, and mention how you heard about the opening or the organization.

(*Middle paragraph*) Explain why you are interested in working for THIS employer, and specify your reasons for desiring this type of work. If you have had experience, be sure to point out your particular achievements or other qualifications that make you a strong candidate. Refer the reader to the enclosed résumé, and restate a few of the most pertinent points on your résumé.

(*Closing paragraph*) Indicate that you wish to meet with the employer to discuss your qualifications and state that you will be contacting the employer within a week. If you can obtain an email address for the employer, you may be more likely to get a response than trying to reach him or her by telephone. Also, give the employer information about how to contact you should he or she desire.

Sincerely,
(*Signature*)
Sara A. Brown

Enclosure (or attachment if sent by email): résumé

3.   The Interview

The interview is the most important step of the job search process. Often a college student's first interview will be with an employer on campus. If the employer has further interest, the student will usually be invited at the employer's expense for a second interview, often called an "on-site" interview if it is conducted at the employer's location.   Whether the interview is on campus, at the employer's facility, or elsewhere, preparation is essentially the same: The student must research the organization. The student who is applying for a particular position should learn as much about the position as possible.   He or she should prepare both answers to questions the employer might ask and questions to ask the employer.

INTERVIEW PREPARATION

Students often underestimate the need for employer and industry research; they may go into the interview having done little or no preparation, thinking that they will be able to "wing it".   Employers, however, can easily spot those students who have not prepared and will generally eliminate them from further consideration.   A recruiter may ask "What do you know about our organization?" Interviewers from the consumer goods industry have asked students to name some of the company's products as a test of their preparation.

Many resources exist to help students with their research.   The first source that students should use is the Internet to search the organization's website. Microsoft's site includes newsgroups, forums, user groups, webcasts, and blogs (web journals).   One job hunter appreciated advice from Gretchen Ledgard, whose blog is about technical careers, stating, "I attribute my recent success as a Microsoft candidate to information I gleaned from your blog." Many companies use blogs to give prospective employees insight into the organization's culture.   Blogs are written by top executives at Sun Microsystems, Boeing, and General Motors, among others. The Internet can also be used to find recent news reports on the organization.

The campus library has many directories such as *Moody's* and *Standard & Poor's*, corporate directories that have information on most large organizations. These directories are also available via the web, however they often require a subscription to access.   Students interested in particular industries should read professional publications in those fields, such as

Advertising Age or *Computer World.* Since many jobs are in the business world, it is a good idea for students to read at least one business publication on a regular basis, such as *The Wall Street Journal, Fortune, Business Week,* or *Forbes.* Contacting friends, former classmates, and alumni who work in the targeted organization or industry is another way to obtain information.

Students should have a good idea of what they want to do for the organization to which they are applying. "I'll do anything" is neither an acceptable nor an honest answer. (Will they really come in at 4:00 a.m. to sweep the floors?) They do not necessarily have to identify a specific job title, but they should be at least able to discuss the skills they have and are interested in using. They might say, for example, "I've always been able to easily establish rapport with people, and I have good communication skills. I am interested in a job in sales"; or, "I am interested in a job that will allow me to use my computer and mathematical skills and my strong analytical ability."

Although employers often want candidates with good interpersonal skills, they hear the phrase "I want to work with people" so often that they dislike it intensely! Job hunters should avoid it.

In addition to having knowledge about the particular organization (and job, if possible), students should have at least a basic understanding of the industry to which they are applying. If interviewing with a health care company, they should read about the health care industry; if applying to a bank, they should know about the various entry-level positions in banking and something about banking in general (including the current prime rate!). It is important to know who the organization's competitors are and any current news about the organization (for example, a recent merger with another company). Students interviewing with publicly traded companies should know the current stock price and if it is on an upward or downward trend.

Preparing for the interview includes rehearsing answers to questions that employers are likely to ask. At the end of this chapter is a list of questions that employers frequently ask college seniors and new graduates. Many employers use an interview approach called targeted selection or behavioral interviewing. In this type of interview, the employer is seeking examples of specific past behavior that relates to particular traits desired. For example, rather than directly asking the student if he or she is creative or has leadership qualities, the interviewer will ask the student, "Give me an example of a time you came up with an innovative approach to a difficult problem," or "Tell me about a time when you exhibited leadership skills."

Some employers, particularly those in the consulting industry, use a method of interviewing called "case interviewing," in which the candidate is given a business problem to solve. Information and the opportunity to practice some case studies may be found on the website of McKinsey & Company, a well-known consulting firm. (See www.mckinsey.com/aboutus/careers/interviewprep/)

Before their interviews students should think about several "war stories" they might tell to demonstrate various traits like leadership, creativity, high achievement, handling failure, and teamwork. They might write these down or rehearse articulating them to you or a friend. Most career offices offer students the opportunity to have a "mock," or practice interview that can be videotaped or recorded on a web camera. After the interview the career counselor critiques the student's verbal and nonverbal behavior. This service is extremely helpful and should be used if available.

Students should prepare questions to ask the employer in order to show interest in the organization and the job. Questions might arise from recent news stories about the organization or might be about the training program, advancement opportunities or attrition rate. Questions about salary and benefits should not be asked; the employer should introduce these subjects first, usually at the offer stage.

INTERVIEW ATTIRE

In general, students should dress conservatively for an interview. Males should wear a navy or charcoal gray suit with a white long-sleeve dress shirt and a traditional tie. A sport coat and slacks are too casual for most interviews. They should wear dark socks (long enough to cover their leg when crossed!) and well-polished black dress shoes. Their hair should be neatly cut. It is strongly advised that they have no facial hair; however, if they choose to have a beard or mustache, it must be immaculately groomed.

For most industries, a conservative haircut (no Mohawks or ponytails) is recommended. The only jewelry acceptable for a male is a watch and a class or signet ring or wedding band, if married. (No gold chains or diamond earrings, please!) According to management surveys by Careerbuilder and Vault, 81 percent of respondents thought that body piercing, other than earrings, left a negative impression; 76 percent felt the same way about visible tattoos.

Females should wear a suit in a conservative color or muted pattern. Recommended colors are black, navy, gray, wine/plum, dark green, and camel. While most employers today consider a pants suit acceptable interview attire for a female, a recent survey of 125 employers revealed that 5% still prefer a skirted suit. Skirts should be slightly above or slightly below the knee. Whether wearing a pants or skirted suit, women should always wear hose (nude-colored) and polished, close-toed pumps with a medium-height heel. If they choose to bring a handbag to the interview, it should coordinate with their outfit and not be oversized. Women should keep jewelry to a minimum (not more than one earring for each ear and no more than a total of three rings on their hands). Long hair should be worn up or held back off the face with a clip.

Students interviewing for positions in artistic, creative or high fashion fields should show more personal flair and fashion awareness in their dress.

Good interview clothes are expensive, costing about $300 - $600 for the complete outfit. Help your son or daughter budget for this in advance, so neither of you will be caught off-guard when it is time to purchase it. (Perhaps this could be a birthday, holiday, or graduation gift.)

Students may want to bring a leather or simulated-leather portfolio and pen to the interview to take occasional notes. (A briefcase is too formal and bulky.) They may use the pen and paper to take a few notes (such as a date to contact the employer or a name and address referred by the employer), but they should avoid writing throughout the interview. They should also bring extra copies of their résumé and a list of their references (with contact information) if the references are not listed on their résumé.

Students also might want to bring samples of their work, if available and relevant for their career field. For example, students interested in advertising should bring a portfolio with some of the campaigns they developed; those seeking positions involving writing should bring clippings of published work.

THE INTERVIEW ITSELF

Students should plan to arrive for the interview about ten minutes early. If the interview is on campus, it is wise to know ahead of time in which building and room the interview will be held. If the interview is at the employer's office or another facility, it is helpful to go there on an earlier day to ensure that it can be found easily. It is the kiss of death to show up late for an interview! If, however, unforeseen circumstances occur - such as a flat tire - that cause a delay, it is essential that the student call and explain the reason for being late.

Some employers also strongly object to an applicant's arriving *too early* for a scheduled interview. So a student who is interviewing at the employer's location and who arrives more than 10 to 15 minutes ahead of time should walk or drive around the block a few times before announcing his or her arrival.

Students should enter the interview room with an air of confidence (but not cockiness). They should greet the interviewer by name and with a handshake. Young women, in particular, are often not yet accustomed to shaking hands. Students should practice a firm handshake. Inserting the web of their hand (between the forefinger and thumb) into the web of the interviewer's hand will ensure that their handshake is firm and not "fishy"— a pet peeve of most employers.

Students should take an active part in the interview and appear animated and enthusiastic. Their answers should be long enough to cover the subject without boring the interviewer. (When the recruiter's eyes begin to glaze over, it's time to stop!) They should give concrete examples that relate to the employer's questions. An easy-to-remember formula is to use the *BAR* approach: when giving an example they should first give the B*ackground* of the situation, then the A*ction* that they took, and finish with the *Result* that occurred.

The student should be sensitive to the interviewer's cues. It is the employer who should lead the interview, setting the pace for the student to elaborate on a response to a question or move on to the next item. If unsure about how much detail to give, the student should give a fairly brief answer and ask if the employer would like more information.

If a student is confronted with a particularly difficult question, it is acceptable to take a moment or two to think before responding. It is far better to ask to come back to it later (since the employer will probably forget) or wait a few seconds, saying something like, "I'd like to think about that for a moment," than to blurt out a quick answer which the student will regret.

Basically the interviewer is seeking to learn whether the student 1) will be able to do the job, 2) will be promotable, 3) will have a positive attitude, and 4) will fit in with the corporate culture. The more preparation the student does before the interview, the better he or she will be able to convince the interviewer of these four things.

Students must not only strive to impress the employer with their verbal responses, they must also be aware of their nonverbal behavior, or "body language". Nervous habits such as twisting a ring, tapping a pencil, or crossing and uncrossing their legs, are distracting to the interviewer. Students should avoid sitting too far forward, very stiffly, or with their hands folded across the chest; on the other hand, a position that is too relaxed comes across as cocky and arrogant. They should make eye contact with the interviewer, but should not stare. (Looking at the interviewer's forehead rather than directly in the eye can ensure this.)

Videotaped or web-cam recorded practice interviews allow students to observe and receive coaching on both their verbal and nonverbal interview behavior.

At the close of the interview, the student should shake the employer's hand and thank him or her for the interview. If the student is still interested in the opportunity, it is important to *clearly state that he or she wants the job and ask the employer to hire him or her for it.* (This feels quite awkward to most students, but is recommended time and again by employers–especially those recruiting for sales positions. Many employers state that this can be the distinguishing factor that determines which students will be offered second interviews.) The student might say, for example, "Ms. Thomas, I am very interested in working for The Widget Company, and I believe that my background is a good fit for this position. I hope you will hire me."

Here are some additional pointers for students regarding the interview:

- Do not denigrate current or former employers or teachers.

- Take an active part in the interview! Be prepared with good questions as well as good answers.

- If the employer hasn't asked about a particular strength or significant experience, find a way to discuss it before the close of the interview (e.g., "There is one more thing I'd like to add before we finish, if I may...").

- Be prepared to discuss weaknesses as well as strengths (a favorite question of many employers), but try to indicate how you are overcoming your weaknesses. Do not volunteer weaknesses, however.

- Do not ask about salary or benefits during the first interview, but have some idea of the appropriate salary range for the position in case you are asked about salary expectations. This information may be obtained from the career office.

- Ask when you might expect to hear further from the employer, if he or she has not indicated a time frame.

QUESTIONS FREQUENTLY ASKED IN AN INTERVIEW

1. Why did you choose this college/university? Why your particular major?

2. What are your short-term and long-term career goals?

3. Which courses/professors have you enjoyed the most? Why?

4. What do you expect to be doing five years from now?

5. Tell me about yourself.

6. What percentage of your college expenses have you financed?

7. Give an example of a crisis situation and how you dealt with it.

8. Give me an example of a time you used your leadership skills. What was the outcome?

9. What has been your greatest challenge thus far? How have you attempted to meet that challenge?

10. Give an example of a time when you failed. What did you learn from the experience?

11. What are your strengths? Your weaknesses?

12. Why are you interested in this organization? Why this position?

13. What do you know about this organization?

14. Give an example of a situation in which you had to manage time effectively (or set priorities).

15. How do you handle rejection? Criticism?

16. Tell me about a situation when you had to be a good team player. Explain your role on the team.

17. Which organizations have you participated in? What have you learned from your involvement?

18. What have you learned from some of the jobs you've had? Under which type of supervisor do you work best?

19. What are your plans for graduate study?

20. What are your geographical preferences or limitations? Are you willing to travel?

21. What two or three things are most important to you to have in your job?

22. Which criteria will you use to evaluate the organizations with whom you are interviewing?

23. How would your friends describe you?

24. What salary do you expect to receive?

25. Why have you chosen this particular career field?

26. With which other organizations are you interviewing?

27. What questions do you have for me to answer?

28. Tell me about a difficult goal you have set for yourself.

THE FOLLOW-UP

Some job seekers have an excellent interview and then shoot themselves in the foot by not following-up afterward. What does follow-up involve? Obviously students should provide the employer with anything requested in the interview. For example, the employer may have asked the student to call the employer's office to arrange to take some type of test, or the employer may have requested that the student have a transcript forwarded by the registrar. These activities should be completed as soon as possible after the interview. Students should always send an email within twenty-four hours thanking the employer for his or her time and expressing continued interest in the organization and position. Some employers recommend following-up the email with a typed letter sent by mail.

If the student has not heard from the employer within a week or two after the time indicated, the student should call the employer to show interest and ask whether any decision has been made. Unless the student is discouraged from contacting the employer or has received a rejection letter, it may be good to email the employer with a brief message or phone the employer every six weeks or so to stay in touch.

SECOND INTERVIEWS

Students who have interviewed on-campus and have successfully made it through the first cut or screening will usually be invited to a second, or even third, interview before a final hiring decision is made. Depending on the employer and the position, these additional interviews may be conducted in the career office, may involve a "day in the field" (during which the student accompanies an employee, such as a sales representative, on the job for a day), or may be scheduled at a regional or corporate office.

Second interviews may involve taking one or more tests that measure an individual's likelihood of success in the position or field. A student may be brought to an organization along with other students whom the employer is considering, and he or she may be asked to participate in several group activities. In these activities the employer is observing the interaction among the students in order to assess an individual's leadership ability as well as teamwork. A student will generally be interviewed by several managers, either individually or in a small group, at a second interview.

Generally the employer will cover all reasonable expenses associated with the second interview. If this has not been stated by the employer, the student should tactfully ask for clarification in advance. ("May I assume that you will be reimbursing me for my expenses?") Most students cannot afford to pay for these (and most parents do not want to!). It is important to get written confirmation by mail, fax, or email indicating which expenses the employer will pay. Some students have learned an expensive lesson that it can be easy to misunderstand which expenses, if any, the employer will be paying.

Students will probably need a credit card to initially charge travel expenses for second interviews; often reimbursement is made by check a few weeks later. Also, many students do not realize the need for traveling with sufficient cash. If they are interviewing in large cities like New York or Chicago, they should take a credit card plus a minimum of $150 cash for two days to pay for taxis, phone calls, tips, and other miscellaneous expenses. They should have an ample supply of $1 bills for tipping.

Students should use good judgment when incurring costs. Occasionally students yield to the temptation of living "high on the hog" on a temporary expense account, and some are simply naive about what is appropriate. One unfortunate student did not realize that the food and drinks stocked in the mini-bar of a posh hotel were not free; the evening before his interview, he invited some of his friends in the area to join him for a party in his room. When he left the city, his room charge, paid by the employer, included a $150 mini-bar tab! The employer paid the bill but informed the director of his career office that the student had just eliminated himself from consideration for a highly prestigious and lucrative job offer. Moral of the story: when in doubt, do not charge it to the employer!

As with the first interview, the student should send an email thank-you letter within twenty-four hours of the second interview, follow-up by a typed mailed letter within three days. If the student has met with several people, he can write to all of them or write to the one or two key individuals and mention the others in the letter.

THE TELEPHONE INTERVIEW

Many employers who do not conduct campus interviews will use a telephone interview for preliminary screening before deciding on the final few to be brought to their location for an in-person interview. Students should prepare for this interview similarly to the way they prepare for the face-to-face interview in terms of researching the organization, anticipating questions they might be asked and that they might want to ask, and having ready a few examples of how they've handled various situations such as challenges, failures, teamwork, and leadership. Some tips for students that apply particularly to the telephone interview are:

- Be sure to be in a quiet, private place when being interviewed by telephone.

- If at all possible, do not use a cell phone, since the reception can be unreliable.

- Disable, or at the very least, ignore, "call-waiting" if another call comes in.

- Keep a pencil and paper handy to take notes.

- Have your résumé and notes with your questions or points that you want to make close at hand.

- If there are several people interviewing you at the same time, ask for each of their names and titles and write them down immediately in the order they are sitting, so you can address them by name as you answer their questions.

- Remember that without nonverbal cues, it is difficult to project both warmth and confidence. To help with these, smile and speak clearly into the telephone; avoid space fillers like "um" and "you know".

- If you are caught off guard by a question, ask for a moment to think about it rather than blurt out the first thing that comes to mind.

- Try to be especially sensitive to talking too much or not answering the question fully. Again, without eye contact and non-verbal cues, it is harder to judge this than in a face-to-face interview. It is fine to stop and ask the interviewer if you should elaborate a bit more rather than going on and on.

- At the conclusion of the interview, thank the interviewer for the time and ask if there any additional information is needed. Be sure to follow-up with an email thank you within a day.

4.   Networking

Job hunting is a contact sport! Throughout this book the importance of making contacts has been stressed. These contacts will be extremely useful to students as they begin their job search.

You can help your son or daughter brainstorm to develop a list of all of the people you know who might be able to assist. The list should include the obvious relatives, neighbors, friends, and co-workers but should also extend to your child's classmates, college teachers, advisers, guest lecturers, and contacts made through participating in career programs, extracurricular activities, and internships and cooperative education experiences. Ask faculty and career services staff where students with the same career goals or from the same academic department have been hired in the past. Contact the alumni chapter closest to your targeted city. If you are a member of a fraternity, sorority, honorary, or professional association, be sure to check these sources for possible networking contacts.

Some relationships start through email, such as a listserv, and can be tapped for job search advice or assistance. One student sighed to her career counselor that "There are no internships related to counseling on eating disorders." The counselor performed a web search for professional associations in this career field. She saw one with a discussion board and looked at a few inquiries. Another college student had just asked about internships and within minutes a member provided a list of employers that had used interns. The same principle can apply to a regular job search–your child should think about networking in the broadest terms.

The concept of networking is, however, much more extensive than using existing contacts. It means making a concerted effort to expand one's immediate circle of contacts. Active participation in student professional associations (including attending conferences if students are allowed), use of the campus alumni connections, and seeking out professionals employed in fields of interest are some ways of doing this.

Students often underestimate their circle of contacts. When asked about their contacts who could be helpful, they generally answer "no one" or come up with a very small list. However, after prodding and coaching, they are astonished to realize how many possible contacts they actually have.

Like most job seekers, students limit their thinking to their "first-level" contacts. That is, they think that in order to get help, they must know a contact that will *directly* lead to a job. However, research shows that it is usually a third- or fourth-level contact who actually results in a job. The source of the job is not the person the job hunter knows, but the person who knows the person who knows the person the job hunter knows!

Imagine a bull's eye, with a student's first-level contacts in the ring immediately adjacent to the bull's eye. When the student asks these contacts for referrals, he or she meets the contacts in the next ring. Asking these second-level contacts for referrals makes contacts in the next ring, or third-level, and so forth. And it is these third- and fourth-level contacts–people the student never knew at the start of the process–who are most likely to be the ones that can lead to a job.

When Selena began seeking a job in publishing she used many avenues. She took advantage of the opportunities that were available through her career office, but few publishers were recruiting on campus. She used the career office, however, to obtain contact information for many publishers, to which she sent cover letters and her résumé. She also spoke to as many people as possible about her desire to find work in the publishing field, preferably as an editorial assistant.

One of the people to whom Selena spoke was a man who had made a presentation at a career panel sponsored by her career office. He indicated that he did not anticipate any openings in his organization, since they were currently going through a downsizing, but he gave Liz the name of a colleague of his at another publishing company whom he thought might be doing some hiring.

Selena contacted this woman, who, in turn, told Selena that her organization was not hiring anyone; but she suggested that Selena get in touch with a friend of hers, who had recently become editor of a small start-up magazine and was looking for a few entry-level people. Selena called the editor, who requested her résumé. A few weeks later Selena interviewed with the editor and shortly thereafter, was hired!

It is important for students to let virtually every one of their contacts know that they are graduating soon and seeking assistance finding a job. Students sometimes are a bit proud about asking for help, or they worry that if they obtain a job through a connection, they will be looked upon as someone who couldn't find a job on their own. But there is nothing at all wrong with using contacts in a job search; in fact, that is the way most people make the initial contact with their employer.

Within two days, students should send a brief email message or typewritten note to each contact used to thank them for their assistance. They should also let them know which job they eventually accept and try to reciprocate in some way.

To spread the word about their job search, some students have business cards printed with their name and contact information and a very brief summary of their credentials. If they have created a website with their résumé, they should also put the URL of this site on their business card. This gives them something easy to carry and distribute at all times in case they meet someone on an airplane, at a conference, or elsewhere. Of course they should also have plenty of résumés on hand, too.

One creative student seeking a position in advertising even had a T-shirt and a bumper sticker for his car printed, advertising his availability! An advertising executive saw it, was impressed with his originality, and hired him!

Developing A Strategy

···

"Cheshire Puss," [said Alice} "...would you tell me, please, which way I ought to go from here?"

"That depends a good deal on where you want to get to," said the Cat.

"I don't much care where___" said Alice.

"Then it doesn't matter which way you go," said the Cat.

"___so long as I get somewhere," Alice added as an explanation.

"Oh, you're sure to do that," said the Cat, "if you only walk long enough."

Lewis Carroll, *Alice's Adventures in Wonderland*

A senior who has been planning ahead should now have a relatively clear focus of his or her initial career goals. This is key to a successful job search; otherwise, a student, like any unfocused job-hunter, will spend a lot of time on activity that is not likely to pay off with satisfying results.

If your son or daughter does not yet have a career direction–or at least a general idea of the type of work he or she wants to do, we recommend returning to some of the suggestions in Chapter 1 regarding career exploration.

Assuming that your senior is ready to move forward on the job search, a written plan of action is recommended. At the end of this chapter is a Senior Job Search Plan Worksheet to help your son or daughter develop his or her own timeline. Although there are some general rules of thumb for most seniors, the time frame of specific activities will vary depending on the individual's career field and prior preparation. The advantages of actually sitting down and writing out a job search plan are 1) breaking down the process into discrete steps makes it appear more manageable, and 2) committing goals to paper results in a greater likelihood of follow-through.

Too many students procrastinate about their job search until late in their senior year, resulting in many missed opportunities.

Finding a job is a job in itself, and it takes time. Unless a student is going to work for a relative or has a job offer from a co-op or internship experience, (which she plans to accept), the job search will probably take many hours. If possible, it is a good idea for a student to plan a fairly light course load during the senior year to allow the necessary time for job hunting.

Seniors should plan a job search strategy that involves activities both in and outside of their career office. They should use directories (both printed and electronic) to make lists of potential employers in their field of interest. Using their contacts, they should attempt to find at least one (preferably several) contact in each organization of interest. They then need to get in touch with their contacts and request help. The help they would most likely need is with information about the organization, tips for getting their foot in the door, names of appropriate contacts within the organization to inquire about entry-level positions, and assistance with obtaining an interview.

Students should set goals for the number of contacts and the number of employers they will contact each week. It is important for job hunters to set goals and stick with them in order not to lose momentum.

After some initial résumés and cover letters have been sent to employers, job seekers need to follow-up by calling or emailing the employers, inquiring whether the letter has been received and, if so, asking for an interview. As mentioned above, it is the interview, rather than the résumé, that leads to a job. (Of course, often the résumé leads to an interview.) Therefore, the student's goal should be to obtain as many interviews with prospective employers in fields of interest as possible.

When contacting employers who do not readily agree to an interview, a bit of persistence–without being obnoxious–can often lead to a face-to-face meeting. For example, if the employer says "We have no openings right now," the student might reply, "I understand that, but I would still like to meet with you for a short time in order to learn more about Company X; I am very interested in working for Company X, and perhaps there will be openings in the future." Although this will not always result in an interview, sometimes it will pay off; in any case the student has impressed the employer with his or her tenacity and interest in the organization.

Most employers are reluctant to agree to an interview if a student is some distance away, since there is usually the assumption that the employer will pay the travel costs. A student who is particularly interested in the employer or in a geographic region might plan (and pay for) a trip to the area and notify employers in advance that he or she will be there during a certain time period. Employers are often receptive to seeing students whose credentials are of interest under these circumstances.

Students should use as many methods of searching for a job as possible and should use all resources available to them. Often students limit themselves to one or two methods: usually campus interviews and internet job postings. Although many students find a job through campus interviews (it varies greatly by major and career field, but the national average is estimated to be about 21 percent), they cannot depend on finding their job this way; and few students are successful with the large internet job boards since the jobs posted often require several years of experience and result in hundreds of responses.

Since it is not possible to predict which of the many job search techniques available will work for any particular individual, the more techniques used, the greater the chance for success.

Job-Hunting Tips

All job hunters want to succeed, yet the degree of success varies tremendously. Why?

Qualifications, the chosen career field, and the amount of career planning activities account for some of the differences, but other important factors are the time, effort, and quality of effort put forth in the job search.

Here are 15 important tips for students looking for a job:

1. Make sure your résumé and cover letter look like they could be published! They must be completely free of typographical, spelling, and grammatical errors and be printed on good quality paper. Do not make extra copies on an inexpensive duplicating machine. Have them professionally done by a copy center. Employers consider your résumé and cover letter an example of your best effort; if they are sloppy, the employer assumes that your work, if you were hired, would be sloppy too.

2. Change the message on your answering machine or cell phone from "Leave your number if you want to party tonight!" to something more appropriate; employers may be calling when you are not in. Be sure that your email address is appropriate ("beach baby@college.edu" is not!).

3. Be immaculately groomed when interviewing. One employer stated to the director of a career office, "When I'm interviewing a candidate, I assume that this is the best he will ever look. It will be downhill from here on."

4. Always prepare thoroughly for interviews; appear eager and interested in the jobs for which you interview.

5. If you are interested in enrolling in graduate or professional at some time in the future, don't mention it in your interview unless you know that the employer encourages it for advancement; employers do not want to invest time and money in training you to have you leave after a short period of time. A major consumer goods company estimates the cost of its year-long management training program to be about $150,000!

6. Follow-up promptly on all correspondence - whether it is a thank you letter after an interview, an invitation for an on-site visit, or a job offer. (Even if you are rejecting an offer, do it promptly; you never know when you might want to re-apply to that organization.)

7. Take advantage of every opportunity you have for a face-to-face meeting with employers, even those in which you have only a mild level of interest. You may learn that a position is more of a fit than you expected.

8. Brush up on your table manners and on business protocol. The interviewing process often involves business meals, cocktail parties,social events, making introductions, and other situations which require rules of business etiquette. (See the Appendix for reference books.)

9. Be as flexible as possible about the position, the size and type of employer, and the place of employment you will consider. Manystudents eliminate excellent opportunities because they do not want to leave their home or college town or want to be near a "special friend". Although this is a choice you have the right to make, you must understand that you may be sacrificing your career (at least initially) for that choice. Other students do not even explore job possibilities with employers whom they do not consider prestigious. (When they are still unemployed four months later, they regret passing up that chance they had to enter a management training program.)

10. Do not overlook opportunities with small organizations. In a survey conducted by Dun & Bradstreet, it was predicted that of three million new jobs to be created, 66 percent were expected to be created by firms with fewer than 100 employees. The nation's largest organizations–those with over 5000 employees–were expected to create only 5 percent of the new jobs.

11. Set your priorities at the beginning of your job search. Few employees can have it all, especially when they are just beginning their career. Determine what is most important to you (such as a challenging job, prestigious employer, high salary, or location) and then go after it.

12. Try to devote some time each day to your job search. Plan to spend 10 to 15 hours a week on it. Do not let a week pass without doing something to further your chances of finding work.

13. Do not relax after applying or interviewing with several employers - even if you feel positive about your chances for a job offer. Many times the offer does not come through. After interviewing and doing the necessary follow-through, assume that you will not receive the job offer, and continue actively pursuing other possibilities.

14. Take advantage of the wealth of information about job-hunting, companies, and employment opportunities listed on the Internet. Depending on mega-job listing sites such as CareerBuilder, Monster, or HotJobs may not result in a job for new graduates.

Niche sites related to a job seeker's career goal or degree may be more helpful. Many job boards or sites (including online newspaper classified ad sections) allow a reader to set up a job search agent. After completing a profile about their background and career interests, he or she can wake up each morning to see matching jobs in email. This service is usually free. The U.S. Department of Labor's Occupational Outlook Handbook (www.bls.gov/oco), the College Board's career information site, (www.collegeboard.com/csearch/majors_careers/profiles/), or Career InfoNet (www.acinet.org/acinet/library.asp?id=14&nodeid=23) can be very helpful in learning about various careers, job functions, and salary information:

Be sure to *always* review the organization's website before contacting them for a job or interviewing.

15. If all else fails, consider temporary employment or volunteer work that will either allow you to develop your skills or to get a foot in the door with an employer of interest, or preferably both.

16. While you may very well want to seek guidance from your parents in your job search, it is important that you come across to an employer as a young adult who can operate independently in the professional world. Never bring your parents to a job interview or have your parents call an employer to discuss an interview opportunity or job offer. A recruiter vented about being approached by parents: "Why on earth do parents call me on behalf of their children? Do they not understand that I'm not interested in working with anyone who lacks initiative to the point that Mommy or Daddy has to call me?"

Safeguarding The Job Search

Unfortunately there are unscrupulous individuals ready to prey on trusting and naïve students while they are in college or seeking a job. It is important for students to use good judgment and to be on the cautious side when putting personal information in any form on the Internet, when revealing information to a potential employer, and when meeting with a purported employer. Specifically, a student should never give out personal information such as social security number, credit card number, and date of birth unless the student is absolutely sure that the employer is legitimate and has a valid reason for requesting this information. Even placing contact information such as telephone number and address on a résumé posted on the Internet can be risky. If in doubt, the student should check with the career office or the student legal assistance office.

A student should only meet with a prospective employer in a public place - never in a hotel room or in a private residence or office that is not in a safe environment. Students must also take precautions in terms of placing revealing photographs or photographs of themselves in compromising positions (partying, using alcohol, etc.) on social networking websites, such as Facebook or MySpace, since employers often find ways to access this information. They should also be very cautious about placing any information that might jeopardize their safety or their chances of being hired by an employer for any reason on such sites. Students often do not realize that not only can employers gain access to this information, but that once information is on the Internet, it is almost impossible to remove it.

Evaluating The Job Offer

Your son or daughter may be among the fortunate students who not only have a job offer but actually have several from which to choose. A fairly common problem for some students with good credentials who have worked hard at their job search is that of "a bird in the hand versus two in the bush".

In other words they have an offer from Company X but they would prefer to work for Company Y, with whom they have interviewed but have not yet heard from. In this situation, the student should try to "stall" Company X by saying something like, "I am very excited about your offer and am pleased that you are interested in hiring me. I am sure that you can appreciate what an important decision this is for me, and I want to be certain that I am making the right one. I would like a bit more time to consider your offer. When do you need an answer?"

If the job offer has been made to the student early in his senior year–before February–the student has more bargaining power in terms of time. Usually the employer will allow the student until close to the end of the fall semester if the offer was made in September-November. For offers extended at the beginning of the spring, the employer is generally willing to wait until March or at least three weeks from the date of the offer for the student to make a decision. However, the later it is in the school year, the more eager the employer is to fill the position, and the more worried she is about losing the best back-up candidates if the student is allowed too long an extension. Even late in the year, though, an employer will typically give the student at least one to two weeks to make a decision. Occasionally an employer will extend what is known as an "exploding job offer" to a student. This means that the offer is only good for a short period of time—perhaps one to two weeks–and will essentially be withdrawn after that. This is considered an unethical practice for an employer of new graduates and should be reported to the career office, who may be able to intervene.

Students in this position should definitely contact other employers with whom they have interviewed and for whom they would prefer to work and let them know of the pending offer. Students must do this in a tactful way so that it does not appear as though they are trying to play one employer against the other or pressure a preferred employer. Nevertheless, it is appropriate for a student to call the preferred employer, explain that there is an offer to which the student must respond by a particular date, and ask if this employer might possibly be able to make a decision about his candidacy by that date. The student should indicate that this employer is his or her first choice, if that is the case. This strategy often is successful in allowing the student to know what his or her options are before making a final decision.

There is no easy formula for determining whether or not a student should accept a job offer. Prior to interviewing, the student should have researched the field well enough to have a sense of the general salary range, benefits, and working conditions typical for the industry, although these will vary by size of employer, geographic region, and other factors.

A student who receives an offer that he or she thinks is inappropriate, because of a very low salary, unreasonable working conditions, or other job considerations, should discuss the offer with a counselor in the career office. The counselor can advise the student about whether to attempt to negotiate with the employer and, if so, how best to approach it.

When considering an offer, students must take into account how likely they are to receive other offers if they decline this one, how flexible they are in terms of location, salary, and other factors, and how much longer they can afford to continue the job search. They should discuss these issues as well with a counselor in the career office.

Some factors to consider before accepting a job offer are:

- Job responsibilities

- Training (both initial and ongoing)

- Salary (and cost of living in geographical area)

- Benefits (including employer match to a 401k plan, company car, or educational assistance)

- Working conditions

- Lifestyle required (e.g., dress code, working hours, travel, etc.)

- Work colleagues (peers and upper management)

A student should carefully weigh a job offer before accepting it. It is considered unethical to accept a job offer and then renege, or back out of the offer, later. Not only is this bad form, it can have negative consequences: the decision may come back to haunt the student, since circles, particularly in some fields, are quite small. The employer with whom a job hunter broke faith today may become his or her boss next year or may be an organization to which he or she wants to apply in five years. And one who reneges may also be denied future use of the career office if the offer was obtained through their services.

Parental Support

How can you as a parent be supportive without being too indulgent? How do you ensure that your son or daughter is doing the necessary job search activity without nagging him or her? It is not easy - but being a parent is not easy. (You already know that!)

Many seniors begin the year enthusiastically seeking a job, but their motivation wanes about halfway through the year, as they realize how much time is involved and how frustrating rejection can be. They often give up at this point, convincing themselves that they will have more time to spend on their job search after graduation. This is a mistake. Interviews are far easier to obtain (though admittedly harder to find time for) while still in school. And employers who are contacted after graduation inevitably want to know why students did not contact them earlier. (They also may have their training classes filled by then.)

When your child becomes discouraged and convinced that "all of this time spent interviewing on campus and contacting employers off campus is useless," remind him or her that it is important to keep working at the job search.

Help your son or daughter keep on track by showing that you are interested in the progress of his or her job search (but not worried about it). When your child is disappointed by the inevitable rejection letters, remain positive. Help him or her realize that almost all students are rejected by some employers and that with persistence, a good job offer is likely to come along.

If your child has put in an adequate amount of time and effort during his senior year (and has done the prerequisite early career planning), he may have a job offer by first semester of his senior year or by graduation, or at least have several good possibilities pending. If not, continue to provide encouragement and suggestions - one of which should be for your child to stay in touch with the career office and have an updated résumé and contact information on file with them.

It is important that your expectations be realistic. According to a survey by NACE, 51.2 percent of college graduates of the class of 2007 had full-time jobs by graduation. Including students who are considering job offers, 81.1 percent have at least one opportunity. Perhaps another 15-25 percent are going directly to graduate or professional school. That means that somewhere between 25-35 percent of new graduates, on average, will not be employed when they graduate college. (Fortunately that figure drops dramatically over time. Approximately 95 percent of new college graduates are employed within a year of graduation.)

Let your child know that you understand that he or she may not be employed by graduation, and provide your child with emotional (and some financial, if possible) support. We do not recommend, however, unconditional and unlimited support: in a positive manner, talk with your child about using the career office, ask which employers he or she has contacted, and ask how he or she is using networking to aid the job hunt.

If your child does not have a job and chooses (with your permission) to return home, discuss the conditions beforehand. You may want to make some new rules now that she is no longer a guest visiting only for holidays and an occasional weekend. Perhaps he or she should do some chores in exchange for room and board. You also may want to discuss your expectations about staying out late or informing you of his or her coming and going. Both you and your child have probably changed significantly during the college years (your child probably more than you). It can be a challenge having an adult child living at home, especially one that you are supporting financially, but setting some ground rules can ease the adjustment for all parties.

Although the particular ground rules are between you and your child, we strongly recommend that one of them be that he or she continue to work on the job search and make daily effort toward it. Many parents are so understanding that there is no incentive for their child to work hard at finding employment. You might consider asking your child to take a part-time or temporary job in order to contribute towards expenses. (But keep in mind that constantly working in an unrelated area will neither help your child gain entry into a chosen field nor allow for time to seek employment.)

JOB HUNTER'S REALITY CHECK

This exercise can help determine how strong a student's qualifications are at a particular point in time to enter the job market. Students should discuss with a career counselor ways to increase strength in areas where scores are low.

Instructions:

1. For each category, select the column to the right that best describes your situation. If you are unsure about some information (e.g., whether your major is high or low demand), talk with a career counselor.

2. Bring the number ("score") over to the far right column.

3. Total all points at the bottom of the next page and refer to scoring scale below.

CATEGORY					# OF POINTS
MAJOR	HIGH DEMAND (10)	NEUTRAL (3)	LOW DEMAND(0)		
CAREER GOAL	HIGH DEMAND (10)	BALANCE BETWEEN SUPPLY & DEMAND (3)	LOW DEMAND, VERY COMPETITIVE (0)	UNSURE OF CAREER GOAL (0)	
GRADES	3.5 & ABOVE (5)	3.0 TO 3.49 (4)	2.6 TO 2.99 (2)	2.0 TO 2.59 (0)	
EXPERIENCE RELATED TO CAREER GOAL (PAID OR UNPAID)	SEVERAL JOBS; CO-OP, INTERNSHIP, VOLUNTEER EXPERIENCEO R PROJECTS (8)	1 TO 2 RELATED EXPERIENCES (5)	NO RELEVANT EXPERIENCE (0)	NOT SURE OF CAREER GOAL (0)	
OTHER (LESS RELEVANT) EXPERIENCE (PAID OR UNPAID)	3 TO 4 JOBS (3)	1 TO 2 JOBS (1)	NONE (0)		
LEADERSHIP ROLES	EXTENSIVE (E.G., ELECTED OFFICER OF STUDENT GROUPS, SUPERVISORY EXPERIENCE ON THE JOB ETC.) (4)	GOOD – MODERATE (1 TO 2 JOBS) (3)	LITTLE TO NONE (0)		

CATEGORY					# OF POINTS
SPORTS ACTIVITIES	TEAM CAPTAIN OF VARSITY SPORTS 2-4 YEARS, SPORTS HONOR ROLL, MVP IN CONFERENCE (4)	VARSITY LESS THAN 2 YEARS, JV, CLUB SPORTS, ETC. (3)	INTRA-MURALS, SOLO SPORTS GOLF, TENNIS, JOGGING (2)	LITTLE TO NONE (0)	
MARKETABLE SKILLS (COMPUTER, ACCOUNTING LABORATORY, ETC.)	EXTENSIVE (8)	GOOD – MODERATE (5)	LITTLE TO NONE (0)		
INTER-PERSONAL SKILLS- (COMFORT LEVEL MEETING, TALKING, WORKING WITH PEOPLE)	VERY COMFORTABLE (5)	SOMEWHAT COMFORTABLE (2)	GENERALLY NOT COMFORT-ABLE (0)		
SOURCE OF COLLEGE DEGREE	VERY PRESTIGIOUS/ SELECTIVE SCHOOL (5)	SCHOOL WITH GOOD ACADEMIC REPUTATION (3)	LESSER KNOWN SCHOOL (1)		
* "WILD CARD" – YOU MAY GIVE YOURSELF 3-6 POINTS IF YOU HAVE ADDITIONAL QUALITIES/SKILLS/FACTORS THAT ENHANCE YOUR CREDENTIALS (E.G., FINANCED 75-100% OF COLLEGE EDUCATION, STRONG NETWORK OF CONTACTS IN DESIRED FIELD; SPECIAL HONORS)				Optional points (3 to 6)	

TOTAL NUMBER OF POINTS	

SCORING SCALE

66-46   Congratulations! You've prepared well and are highly competitive. Nevertheless, in today's job market even students with the best credentials need to work hard at finding a job.

45-25   Your credentials to compete for a job are good to moderate. Be thorough and persistent about all aspects of your job search. Don't overlook opportunities to work for smaller, lesser-known organizations. Use informal contacts at career fairs and panels to impress recruiters with your interpersonal skills, since your résumé may not be strong enough to get the interviews you desire.

24-0   Your credentials in the job market are not especially strong. You may want to "beef them up" by taking some course work in areas sought by employers (e.g., accounting, business, or computer science), obtaining part-time work (either paid or unpaid) or involving yourself in campus organizations. Plan to put extra effort into your job search, and don't concentrate on prestigious employers. (Many less glamorous jobs and organizations offer excellent training opportunities.)

PRATAP GUPTA
pgupta@nc.rr.com
708-555-2000 (cell)

Temporary Address	**Permanent Address**
P.O. Box 3462	1406 Claremont Avenue
Boston, MA 02128	Northbrook, Il 60062

OBJECTIVE: A position as a sales management trainee

EDUCATION: **Queens College, Boston, MA**
Bachelor of Arts, English, June 2008
GPA: 3.2   Dean's List-4 semesters
Study Abroad Program in Seville, Spain, Summer 2007

RELATED   **PHONATHON**, Queens College Development Office, Boston, MA
EXPERIENCE: **Supervisor**, September 2007-present
- Trained and motivated 100 student callers in alumni solicitation; generated $1,000,000 in donations, an increase of 15% over 2006

Fundraiser, October 2006-April 2007
- Raised over $6,000 for the College; promoted to supervisor

ARTECH CORPORATION, Princeton, NJ
Marketing Assistant, July-September 2007
- Promoted new products through e-marketing campaign.

QUEENS STUDENT CREDIT UNION
Marketing Division Committee, September 2006-May 2007
- Targeted marketing strategies to sophomore and junior classes.

DUPLEX PRODUCTS, INC. Chicago, IL
Sales Representative, May-September 2006
- Made telemarketing calls using sales strategies; exceeded quota.
- Wrote sales letters to prospective clients.

QUEENS MARKETING ASSOCIATION, Boston, MA
Publicity Committee, Fall 2005
- Advertised Marketing Association and increased membership
- Identified and invited guest lecturers to discuss career options.

OTHER   **Sales Associate**, Marshall Fields, Oakbrook, IL
EXPERIENCE: **Waiter**, The Rathskeller, Boston, MA

ACTIVITIES: **Beta Theta Pi Fraternity**, Social Chairman, Songleader
Senator, Morrison Residence Hall

SKILLS: Excel, Access, MS Word, SAS; fluent in Spanish

REFERENCES AVAILABLE UPON REQUEST

217

SENIOR JOB SEARCH PLAN WORKSHEET

··

August-September

- Draft or update résumé by (date) _____
- Have critiqued by career office by_____
- Have copies printed by_____
- Register or update profile with career office by _____
- Attend career office interviewing and job-seeking workshops by

  _____

- List possible useful contacts (to be added to as additional ones become known)

  _____

  _____

  Other activities:

  _____

  _____

  _____

September-November

- Meet with campus career counselor by_____
- Schedule practice interview with career office by _____
- Check list of campus recruiters and attempt to schedule interviews with:

  _____

  _____

- Research employers before interviewing.

  _____

- Write follow-up letters to the following employers:

    Interview with_____on_____; send follow-up by_____

    _____

    _____

- Attend career fair(s) on _____
- Attend career panels/programs on

    _____

    _____

December-January (Holiday Break):

- List employers to contact (who are not scheduled to recruit on-campus)
    Contact _____by_____

    _____

- List networking contacts to write or call:
    Contact _____by_____

    _____

- Second interviews scheduled with the following employers

    _____

Mid-January-March:

- Schedule visit with campus career counselor to discuss
    progress:_____

- Continue on-campus interviews. Attempt to schedule with:

- Follow-up with employers from campus interviews and other contacts:

Contact _____ by _____

_____

_____

Mid-March:
- Second interviews with:

_____

- Attempt to schedule interviews with employers not recruiting on campus:

  Contact _____ by _____

  _____

  _____

- Call new and previous networking contacts to keep in touch:

  Contact _____ by _____

  _____

  _____

• Use other methods of job-seeking (Internet listings, classified ads, professional journals, etc.):

_____

_____

April-May:
- Schedule visit with career counselor to discuss progress

  by _____

- Continue to network with contacts:

  Contact _____ by _____

  _____

  _____

- Make appointment to discuss offers (if any) with career counselor:

  _____

June-Acceptable Job Offer:

- Ensure résumé and contact information are on file with career office before leaving campus.

- Continue employer and network contact:

  Contact _____ by _____

  _____

  _____

- Continue other avenues of job-seeking (classified ads, professional journals, Internet, etc.). List:

  _____

  _____

  _____

  _____

  _____

Summary

··

Basic Tools Of The Job Search

The Résumé

- Develop a draft based on recommended guidelines

- Have draft critiqued by career office adviser

- Have copies professionally printed on good quality paper

The Cover Letter

- Use recommended format and have first one critiqued by a career services counselor

- Address the letter to a specific person

- Tailor letter to each organization

- Emphasize the contribution that can be made to the employer

- Use active approach in closing

The Interview

- Prepare thoroughly by researching the organization

- Prepare good questions in advance

- Schedule a practice interview with a career counselor

- Dress properly for the interview

- Show energy and enthusiasm in the interview

- Attend to both verbal and non-verbal behavior

- Always follow-up promptly after the interview

Networking

- Develop and use contacts

- Do not limit contacts to immediate circle

- Send an email or typed thank-you letter to each contact used within one week and notify them when you have accepted a job.

Developing A Strategy

- Determine priorities

- Remain flexible

- Develop a plan and timetable for job search activities

- Do something each week on the job search

- Use as many resources as possible

Parental Support

- Have realistic expectations

- Show an interest in your child's job search

- Give encouragement and support

- Help keep motivation up

- Set guidelines and limits for financial support

- Establish ground rules for adult children returning home

Conversation Starters For Parents And Students

1. What are your major priorities for your first job after college?

2. What type of timetable do you think will work best for you for your job search? Have you worked on a detailed job search plan?

3. Have you started working on your résumé? I'd like to work on it with you. Have you shown it to a counselor at your career office? What suggestions did they make for improvement?

4. Have you drafted a basic cover letter? Has your career office reviewed it and made any suggestions for changes?

5. What kinds of questions are you anticipating from employers who will be interviewing you? Which questions have you prepared?

6. Have you checked with your career office to see if they offer practice interviews? Would you like me to role-play an interview with you (or have you role-played an interview with a friend)?

7. Shall we brainstorm together about our possible contacts who may be helpful with your job search?

8. Do you want to use spring break to job hunt in another city or state?

CHAPTER 9

MAKING THE MOST OF THE COLLEGE CAREER OFFICE

Making allowances for exaggeration, one could say that many college seniors approach their career office as they would a fast-food restaurant: "I'll have one of those biggie jobs with a large order of benefits and some perks on the side." They expect to wait about five minutes (certainly no more than five days) for their order to be filled. Students–as well as parents–can be quite unrealistic about the role of the career office in the job search process.

What responsibility does the career office have to help your child find a job?

The vast majority of college career offices view their role as primarily an educational one. They do not consider themselves employment agencies; in fact, almost all have taken the word "placement" out of their office name, feeling it gives students the impression that the office will secure a job for them.

The mission statement of the career office of the University of North Carolina at Chapel Hill is a fairly typical one: "The mission of University Career Services is to provide progressive services and resources that help students choose and prepare for their careers, learn job search skills, and find employment." Note the emphasis on providing *services* and *resources* and on *helping* students find employment, rather than finding it for them.

Most career offices are staffed by dedicated, competent career counselors and advisers who are well-trained and knowledgeable. They generally have advanced degrees and experience outside an educational setting. They can be very helpful to your son or daughter in every stage of the job search. However, they are not magicians. It is not possible for them to wave a magic wand over the résumé of a senior with a low grade point average and three years of experience as a lifeguard, restaurant server, and sales clerk and create a résumé that will dazzle employers and result in several job offers!

The career office attempts to help underclassmen understand the need for early career planning. In addition to educating students about how to research and plan for their career, the office teaches job search skills and provides linkages with employers.

Career offices advertise their services through various means: an Internet home page, email messages to students, the school newspaper, fliers and posters, newsletters, and possibly even individual letters to you or your student. However, unless your child is enrolled at a very small school, the career office is not likely to have the resources to personally seek out your son or daughter and ask why he or she has not yet used the career office.

It is your child's responsibility to take advantage of the many programs and services offered and to use them well before the senior year. Students who do no preparation for their career and wait until the last possible moment to seek assistance from the career office cannot expect miracles— nor can their parents. Some students do not even visit the career office until after graduation, when they are suddenly panic-stricken. Of course by then all of the recruiters who were interviewing on campus have long since come and gone, and the jobs they were offering have been filled by students who began interviewing as early as September or October of their senior year.

At one time the career office of The University of Nebraska at Lincoln posted a sign that read, "Coming to Career Services after graduation is like studying for finals after the exam"!

When To Go

Students should begin using their college career office no later than their sophomore year. Ideally they will visit the office on a regular basis, getting to know at least one or two of the career advisers and, equally important, ensuring that these advisers know them. Even at very large institutions, it is possible for your son or daughter to develop a close enough relationship with some of the professional staff to be remembered by them from one visit to the next. If your child is known by the staff, he or she is more likely to be referred when the office receives a job opening that is a perfect match or when an employer asks for the recommendation of a few qualified students.

Occasionally the career office seeks students for unique or one-time opportunities, such as helping an employer with a presentation, conducting student or employer surveys, etc. The office is likely to call upon students they know for these opportunities, which can develop into valuable contacts and job leads.

Alec was a sophomore interested in exploring career counseling as a career. He volunteered with his campus career office to do any work needed–clerical, computer data entry, library assistance–whatever. After a few months, he was appointed to the career services' advisory board, which included students, faculty, and employers.

He also was asked to help with career panels, hosting employer speakers. Through his work in the career office, he had many conversations with the staff about career options; he eventually decided to combine his interest in career counseling with an interest in business and seek a career in human resources.

Utilizing an employer contact from the career office advisory board, Alec obtained an internship in human resources with a small company for the summer following his sophomore year. That internship, along with school activities the following year, led to another internship the next summer, this time with a large organization. As a senior, Alec had strong credentials (not to mention strong advocates at the career office!) which led to several job offers in his chosen field.

When senior year arrives, encourage your child to meet with a career counselor soon after returning to campus in the fall and to continue meeting regularly with the counselor throughout the year. Students planning to graduate in December should begin using the career office for employment assistance two semesters before graduation. Both underclassmen and seniors should use the many programs and services offered through the career office discussed later in this chapter.

To be effectively served by the career office, students must follow through on their responsibilities, such as registering for services in a timely manner (usually required for internship assistance, on-campus interviewing, and résumé referral), keeping the résumé and profile they have online with the career office up-to-date, and checking with the office to ensure that their letters of reference have arrived.

Whom to See and What to Ask

Many career offices have "walk-in" or "drop-in" hours, generally intended for quick questions; students may be limited to a short period of the counselor's time during the walk-in period. "Walk-ins" are best used for a final review of a résumé or cover letter or for questions that can be easily and quickly answered, such as about the salary range needed to be competitive for a given occupation or proper dress for an employer reception.

For anything other than a quick question, it is better for students to schedule an appointment in advance to be assured of meeting with the right staff member for their needs and of having adequate time to discuss their situation.

Many career offices assign professional staff to particular levels of students (such as underclassmen, seniors, etc.) or to specialty areas (such as liberal arts, engineering, etc.). When visiting the career office students should explain the reason for their visit to the receptionist and ask which staff member might be best to see.

Your son or daughter will get more out of the visit and reduce the chances of being told to come back to see a different staff member ("who is more knowledgeable about internships," etc.) if he or she is as specific as possible when making the appointment. Your child might say, "I'm a sophomore thinking about a career in computer graphics, and I'd like to talk with someone who can help me prepare for a career in this field," or "I am a junior business major and would like to schedule an appointment with a counselor who can help me search for a summer internship related to finance."

Some career offices now offer students the opportunity to select the most appropriate counselor from information on the website and to schedule an appointment online.

You may have a son who, like many students, avoids visiting the career office because he is so unsure of a career choice that he does not even know what to ask and is concerned about looking foolish. You can help allay these fears by explaining that the career office exists to help students at all levels of career preparation. Although on some campuses it may be the function of the counseling center rather than the career office to work with unfocused students, all campuses provide assistance with career choice: it is just a matter of finding the correct office, and the career office is usually a good starting point. Your child should simply state the truth: "I'm clueless about choosing a career."

Or, perhaps you have a daughter who is at the other extreme: she may be so certain of her goal ("I'm going to medical school") that she assumes that as long as she is taking the necessary courses and doing well academically, there is no need to talk with a career counselor. Most of the time, however, a counselor can provide information that will be helpful, perhaps even critical, for meeting that goal. For example, the counselor might explain that paid or volunteer experience in the health field is virtually a necessity for consideration by medical schools. Additionally, since students' plans often change either by choice or necessity, a counselor can discuss how and why a student should develop a backup plan.

Most students are actually somewhere in the middle of the spectrum of deciding on a career; these students often wait to visit the career office until they have a specific reason, such as seeking an internship. This is fine if the reason arises early in the student's college years, but a student who feels there is no need to use the career office until late in senior year could miss out on much-needed information and help.

Five Myths About Career Offices

1. Myth - The career office is only helpful for (business, engineering, computer science, etc.) majors.

Fact - The career office can help all majors, although it cannot always provide the same services to all. Campus recruiting, for example, is primarily a function of employer demand rather than career office effort or preference. If your child is interested in a career in broadcasting, for example, chances are high that there will be few, if any, campus interview opportunities for him, simply because the broadcasting industry does not typically conduct campus recruiting.

Nevertheless, many broadcasting stations list job openings with career offices, so a résumé may be sent by the career office in response to these listings. There are many other ways the career office can help all students, regardless of their major or career interest, such as helping them prepare to be a strong candidate for their chosen field, teaching them job search skills, and providing directories and databases of potential employers and alumni contacts (many of these are online).

2. Myth - The career office is for seniors.

Fact - This book has emphasized the need for students to visit their career office by their sophomore year. Virtually all career offices provideindividual career counseling, career planning workshops, internship assistance, and career fairs and programs - all services for underclassmen.

Many also offer assistance with finding a part-time job, choosing a major, and assessing interests. These, too, provide reasons for a freshman or sophomore to make use of the career office.

3. Myth - Many employers who conduct campus interviews are not really hiring.

Fact - Campus interviewing is very expensive for employers. Organizations are not willing to spend time and money on transportation, hotel and meal costs, and lost work time just for public relations purposes. Employers who are interviewing almost always intend to hire, although in some cases they are not sure of the exact number or location of the jobs that will be available upon graduation. This is particularly true of large organizations that can predict that they will have sales openings, for example, but cannot predict in October or January specifically where the openings will be in May or June. Although employers visiting a particular campus do intend to consider students from that campus for positions (otherwise they would not be recruiting there), some employers are extremely selective; they may interview as many as 500 students for 10 or 12 openings, resulting in their not making a job offer to any student from some of the campuses they visit.

4. Myth - Employers interviewing on campus only hire students with at least a 3.0 GPA.

Fact - Some organizations *do* use a GPA cutoff - in fact some, like investment banks or prestigious technical companies, have a cutoff much higher than a 3.0. Most organizations, however, consider a student's overall background, including work experience, extracurricular activities, and demonstrated leadership skills. Some employers stress these factors much more than grades. Your son or daughter should discuss his or her strengths and interests with a career counselor in order to best determine which employers and industries to target.

5. Myth - Very few students get a job through career services.

Fact - What constitutes "getting a job"? Most career offices offer many services and provide assistance in many different ways, all serving to enhance the student's job-seeking skills. This can include a great deal of indirect help, such as critiquing résumés or practice interviews, that eventually pays off. The career office may sponsor a career fair at which a student makes a contact eventually resulting in a job offer; or a career counselor may provide the student with the name of an alumnus working in the student's desired career field, which may prove to be a successful job lead.

Effectively Using Career Office Programs And Services

Although there is some consistency among programs and services offered by career offices, there are also a great many differences: offices vary tremendously in terms of staff size, staff-student ratio, budgets, facilities, philosophy, technology, innovation, and other characteristics. Listed below are programs and services that exist at some, but not necessarily all, career offices. You and your son or daughter may want to call or visit the career office in your child's freshman or sophomore year to inquire about the services offered. You certainly should view their website. (Some prospective college students and parents are even investigating the services of the career office prior to selecting a college.)

Career counseling

As has been previously mentioned, your child should meet periodically with the career adviser for his or her major or interest area. Students often wrongly assume that counselors are too busy to see them (especially on large campuses) and never check, losing out on the opportunity available for individual help. They miss out on the chance for expert advice at no charge. Many, upon graduating without a job or direction, realize they need professional help and may then have to pay as much as $75-$150 an hour for private career counseling.

Interest testing and computerized guidance programs

Most campuses offer career guidance for undecided students. Assistance may be provided through counseling, interest testing, and - an increasingly popular option - computerized programs that are often available via the office website. These services may be provided by the career office or the counseling center, depending on the particular college or university. If your son or daughter is unsure of a major or career choice, he or she should inquire at the career office about available help.

Career fairs and programs

Your child should check the career office website in August or September to view the schedule of programs for the year or at least for the fall semester. (Most career offices plan far in advance.) He or she should mark these programs on the calendar so as not to forget them. Career fairs, career panels, and other career programs are important ways for students to learn about occupations, how to prepare for them, and to make valuable contacts. Students should participate in these programs each year, starting as a freshman or sophomore.

Career planning and job search workshops

Most career offices offer workshops on planning for a career, obtaining an internship, résumé-writing, interviewing, and job search strategies. This information is often available on the career office website as well, although attending a workshop has the advantage of allowing the student to ask questions and to meet career office staff. Some offices have workshops on specialized topics such as business etiquette, networking, and employment trends. Encourage your child to attend as many workshops as possible. These are valuable services that may prove costly if your child is interested in them following graduation.

Career planning course (for academic credit)

Many colleges and universities offer a career planning course for credit, often taught by staff of the career office. Such a course is especially useful for undecided students, but can be helpful for all students. Since students often put off planning for their career and doing the requisite research and activities, a course can help ensure that these activities get done.

Cooperative education and internship assistance

Almost all schools provide help to students desiring internships, and many have co-op programs. Your son or daughter should check with the career office early in the fall of sophomore and junior years to learn about the services available for experiential learning (co-op and internship experiences). Again, students cannot expect to necessarily be placed in a co-op or internship by the career office, but they should receive help conducting a campaign to search for the position (including help with writing a résumé, interview tips, directories of employers, position listings, etc.). Many career offices have campus interviews and a résumé-referral service for co-op and internship positions.

Externships/Job-shadowing programs
Students may have the opportunity through their career office to have a short-term experience observing someone doing the type of work in which they are interested. Externships, sometimes called job-shadowing programs, generally take place over fall or spring break or at another time when students are free from class. (Some schools, such as Dartmouth College, have a three-week free period in January–"the Jan term"–during which students often participate in externships.)

Resource room/Career library
Almost all career offices have a resource room, or career library, although some will be more extensive than others. In the career library your son or daughter will find information about many occupations and job search skills. An increasing number of career offices now have many of these resources available on computer. Some career offices have their library staffed with an employee or student helper, but many are designed for self-help. If your child is confused by the organization of the library or cannot find the necessary information, by all means have him ask for assistance. Unfortunately, many students become discouraged when they cannot find the resource they need, and leave without requesting help.

Alumni databases
Students can usually obtain contact information for alumni working in various fields through their career office. This information is generally available online via the career office website, making it easy for students to search by various criteria, such as "alumni/ae working in publishing in Boston". These alumni have volunteered to help students and are eager to be contacted, yet students sometimes complain that they contact alumni and do not hear back from them. It is suggested that students email alumni in order to make it as easy as possible for them to respond.

Practice (mock) interviews
If the career office offers the opportunity for students to have a mock, or practice, interview, your child should schedule one. Many offices have the capability to record the practice interview with a videotape or web camera. This service is one of the most valuable learning experiences for job hunters, yet it is widely underused. Perhaps students are embarrassed to

have their mistakes captured on video or they are simply unaware of the service; in any case, those students who do take advantage of this service consistently rate it as highly valuable. It is far better for a student to look foolish in a practice interview with a counselor than in a real interview for a job!

Campus interviews

Students and their parents often focus almost exclusively on the number and type of employers interviewing on campus. Campus interviewing is certainly convenient for students and is productive, if only because it gives them an opportunity to hone their interviewing skills; however, many students will not obtain a job through this method. Many industries do not conduct any campus interviews; and hiring for many jobs, such as public relations or non-profit work, is rarely done through campus recruiting.

Students should view campus interviewing as one of the many services provided by the career office that can help them in their job search. (Occasionally there are campus interviews for cooperative education or internship positions as well.) They should not look at campus interviews as an all-or-nothing situation: that is, they should not put all of their eggs in this one basket, expecting to find a job through campus interviews and doing nothing additional in their job search. But neither should they summarily dismiss campus interviews as having nothing for them! Encourage your son or daughter to register with the career office in order to be eligible to interview and to regularly check the schedule of employers visiting campus. They may be quite pleasantly surprised to see employers as diverse as Neiman Marcus, Bank of America, Teach for America, Target, IBM, and Kraft Foods recruiting on their campus. The number and type of employers recruiting will greatly depend on the job market as well as the size of the college or university, its reputation among employers, and its production of graduates with the academic preparation and other qualifications sought by employers.

Career offices use various methods for student interview sign-up. Because more students may be interested in interviewing with an employer than interview slots available, usually the employer will select the students to be interviewed (generally from résumés submitted by the student in advance of the employer visit), or the career office may select the candidates from a bidding, lottery, or other system. If your son or daughter is having difficulty obtaining interviews with desired employers, he or she should discuss this with a counselor. There are often ways around "the system," such as contacting the employer by email or phone and requesting consideration.

Employer databases

Many career office libraries, especially on large campuses, subscribe to employer databases in order to make available to students information on many different organizations. One employer database, Career Search, contains information on nearly a million employers, which can be searched by such characteristics as industry, location, or size of employer. These databases do not have job openings (much to students' dismay), but they are extremely useful for developing lists of employers to target and for obtaining brief employer profiles.

Résumé-referral service

Many employers, particularly small ones, do not have the budget or staff available for campus recruiting; additionally, they may have a need for only one or two employees and may need these employees immediately. These employers will often contact the career office and request the office to send them résumés of qualified students. Some large career offices may receive as many as 2,000 or more job requests a year.

It is definitely to your child's advantage to inquire about this service and the requirements for participation. Generally, he will need to register with the career office and place a résumé in the career office's database. Often students do not realize that the majority of résumé-referral activity takes place in late spring or summer, just before or after graduation. They may submit their résumé to the career office early in their senior year and become discouraged if they are not contacted by employers. However, if students are graduating without a job, it is important to stay in touch with the career office, letting the office know that they wish to be referred for any positions that might relate to their interests. They must be sure that the career office has a current copy of their résumé on file, giving an address and telephone number where they can be reached once they leave campus.

Reference service

Fewer and fewer career offices maintain reference files for all students because many employers wish to directly contact references rather than receive a copy of a written letter on file with the career office. Nevertheless, this service is available on some campuses for either all students or for those with specialized needs, like students applying to graduate or professional school or students in particular majors, such as education or health sciences. This service is convenient for students, since it allows them to have their letters of reference on file at the career office. They can then request that the letters be sent by the office each time they apply to a graduate or professional school. The reference service eliminates the need to contact their references each time they need a letter and ensures that the letters will be sent in a timely manner. Even if your child does not expect to need references until several years later (e.g., for graduate or professional school), he or she should obtain them before leaving campus. Faculty members can write a stronger recommendation when a student's performance is recent. Also, it may be difficult to locate professors who have moved to another institution or retired. There is typically a fee to establish a reference file and an additional fee for each mailing. Your son or daughter should ask if this service is available. If it is not, there are private firms, such as Interfolio and ReferenceNow, that offer these services to individuals for a fee.

Internet home page
The career office's home page offers a wealth of information and should be visited on a regular basis. This is where students will find basic information on all of the services and programs offered as well as material on writing résumés, interviewing tips, job search etiquette, and much more. The career office home page will also link to other valuable job search resources available on the Internet.

Job listings
All career offices post job listings on their website. These listings may include permanent, summer, part-time, internship, and cooperative education positions. Your child should check the openings frequently.

Graduate and professional school advising
This service may be a function of the career office on some campuses, whereas on others it is handled by another department, possibly in the graduate school or the office of academic advising. If your child has an interest in further education, he or she should find out which office handles advising and begin talking with a graduate school adviser by sophomore year or as soon as his or her interest develops.

Graduate and professional school fairs and forums
Many career offices also sponsor graduate and professional school fairs and forums. These are programs attended by admissions representatives from

many educational institutions. The programs may be dedicated to one professional specialty, such as law or business schools, or may be of a general nature, with representatives, for example, from many graduate schools across the country. Students should not wait until their senior year to attend these programs, since the information they glean from the representatives can be invaluable for preparing adequately for admission. The admissions representatives can provide information on desired major, work experience, course work, grades, and other qualities needed to be a competitive candidate for acceptance to their school. If your child has even the slightest interest in graduate or professional school, he or she should check with the career office about these programs.

First Destination surveys and statistics
It is helpful for your son or daughter to know what graduates of his or her school and major have done after graduation. The career office should be able to provide this data from surveys, often called first destination surveys. Of course, statistics can never predict what will happen to any one individual - your child may be the one journalism major who is hired directly out of school by the *Wall Street Journal* at a starting salary of $45,000; however, statistics can help to realistically set expectations about salary, length of time to find a job, type of employment, and sources leading to employment in a particular field. Do not wait until the senior year to request this information from the career office; it can be a valuable resource for making academic and career decisions throughout college.

Alumni services
Most career offices provide services to graduates for at least six months after graduation without charge. Beyond that, offices vary in terms of the length of time a graduate may use the office and fees (if any) charged; some career offices allow alumni to use their services indefinitely, whereas others may have a cut-off point of one to five years after graduation. The university alumni office will generally offer career assistance to graduates who are no longer eligible to use the career office.

Conclusion

If used early, effectively, and often, the career office can be extremely helpful to your son or daughter in his or her job search. Most offices are happy to answer questions from interested and concerned parents. Remember, though, that your child must take responsibility for planning for a career and for putting forth the effort that it takes to find a job. Neither you nor the career office can or should do that; but with your support, the career office's assistance, and your son or daughter's commitment, your child should be able to attain at least a start towards his or her career goal.

Summary

....

Realistic Expectations Of The Career Office

The career office:

- Can provide services and resources to help students

- Can provide individual assistance to students

- Is not responsible for finding a job for students

When To Go

Students should:

- Visit the career office by their sophomore year

- Use the career office frequently

- Begin using the career office at least two semesters before graduation for employment assistance

Whom To See/What To Ask

Students should:

- Be as specific as possible about their needs when making an appointment

- Request to see the counselor for their major or career interests

- Be candid with the career counselor about their needs

Five Myths About Career Offices

- The career office is only helpful for certain majors
- The career office is only for seniors
- Many employers interviewing on campus are not hiring
- Most employers interviewing on campus require a 3.0 GPA
- Very few students get a job through career services

Career Office Programs And Services

- Individual career counseling
- Interest testing and online career guidance programs
- Career fairs and programs
- Career planning and job search workshops
- Career planning course for credit
- Cooperative education and internship assistance
- Externship/job shadowing programs
- Resource room/career library
- Alumni databases
- Practice (mock) interviews
- Campus interviews
- Employer databases
- Résumé referral service
- Reference service
- Internet home page
- Online job listings
- Graduate/professional school advising

- Graduate/professional school fairs & forums

- First Destination surveys/statistics

- Alumni services

Conversation Starters for Parents and Students

....

1. Have you checked with the career office to learn about the services they offer for underclassmen? For seniors? Please tell me about them.

2. Which of the services and programs of the career office do you think will be most useful to you? Why?

3. Which employers are coming to campus to interview this year? With whom would you like to interview?

4. Have you looked at the First Destination surveys of past graduates? What types of jobs have other graduates in your field found, and what were the typical salaries? Which organizations have hired them? Which graduate or professional schools admitted them?

5. Have you met with the career counselor for your major or career interests? What advice did he or she provide? Are you regularly using this counselor as a resource for your questions about career planning and your job search?

CHAPTER 10

Information For Special Populations

While the information in this book applies to virtually all students and parents, this chapter addresses the unique needs and resources that pertain to particular groups such as African-Americans, Hispanics, and other racial and ethnic minorities; gay, lesbian, bisexual, and transgender students; international students; students with disabilities; and female students.

Students in these special population groups may find it valuable to connect with mentors and experienced professionals in fields that interest them who are members of the same group. Most career offices can help students make these connections, generally through an alumni database.

Useful resources are listed at the end of the chapter.

Minorities

As with all students, it is recommended that minority students register with the career office by their sophomore year and investigate internship programs well before their senior year. Minority students may find it interesting and helpful in their adjustment and enjoyment of college to join and take an active role in campus minority organizations such as The Society of Black Engineers, the Black Business Student Alliance, the Black Student Movement, the campus Hispanic Association, the Society of Hispanic Engineers, etc. These groups can be career enhancers as well, since many are career-related and bring in speakers to discuss career options, give advice, and consider students for internship and employment opportunities. Some professional associations, such as the American Indian Science and Engineering Society, have openings for national and regional student representatives. These students have high visibility roles with the organization's officers and may have travel expenses paid to attend national conferences.

Students may also use Chambers of Commerce for resources on special populations. These resources are organized by geographic location (national, regional, local) and special population. Some examples include the United States Hispanic Chamber of Commerce (www.ushcc.com) and the National Gay and Lesbian Chamber of Commerce (gaylife.about.com/od/gayatwork/).

Many career offices have staff designated to work with diverse populations and offer programming and resources for minority students such as diversity career fairs, special internship opportunities, and leadership programs that target minority students. Encourage your child to investigate what is available. Some particularly helpful publications that may be in the career office resource room are the magazines *The Black Collegian* and *Job Choices –Diversity Edition* (published by the National Association of Colleges and Employers) and books listed in this chapter's Resources section.

Minority students sometimes inquire about whether or not they should reveal their minority status on their résumé or when registering in the career office database. While this is certainly an individual decision, the authors would recommend doing so in most instances, since employers often express to the career office their interest in diversifying their hiring. They are especially eager to ensure that minority students are aware of and apply for positions with their organization. In order to accomplish their goals, these employers may designate some internships, leadership and special programs, and scholarships for minority students.

Your child should inquire about these opportunities. By indicating on the résumé that the student has participated in campus groups such as the Black Student Movement, or Hispanic Association, the student informs the employer about both minority status and leadership activities.

Some cultures have particularly close family ties, and parents from these cultures may be especially reluctant to have their children participate in a study abroad program or take a summer internship far from home. It is important for parents to consider the fact that their children are likely to develop independence and personal growth as well as career-related experience through these opportunities, all of which will be valuable to their future.

Minorities and women are underrepresented in technical fields and can benefit from special programs designed to encourage their entry into careers such as science, engineering, mathematics, and technology. The federal government is hiring a high volume of new college graduates in the next five years due to expected retirements of baby boomers. Many programs are targeted to students in special populations, such as women, minorities, and students with disabilities (www.studentjobs.gov/).

Graduate and professional programs are also targeting special groups. Eleven universities have expanded premedical and predental programs designed for minority students to include economically disadvantaged students, those from rural areas, and populations that have been underserved in health care. The Summer Medical and Dental Education Program (www.smdep.org/background.htm) is promoted to eligible freshmen and sophomores.

African-Americans

Many minority students are typically interested in social services and health-related careers. Parents of minority students often encourage them to attend professional school in medicine and law. However, students should consider all their possible options. Businesses and government agencies target scholarships and internships to minorities who are underrepresented in science, technology, engineering, and mathematics careers.

African-American students who are excelling academically may be encouraged to help the admissions office recruit high school students from under-represented groups. Successful students may also have opportunities to advise, mentor, or tutor other minority students or volunteer to participate in activities for at-risk children. Your child may be eager to inspire others to enter college and set ambitious goals for themselves. These activities are commendable and help build leadership skills. However, they are no substitute for career-related internships and work experience (unless, for example, your son or daughter wants to enter the field of education).

A growing area in business is multicultural marketing. For example, The Walt Disney Company has job openings in Urban Marketing and Hispanic Marketing. Members of minority groups can bring a unique perspective to these types of positions. The American Advertising Federation (AAF) offers special programs to minority students through MOSAIC.

Students should research a prospective employer's record on hiring and promoting a diverse workforce. Many publications develop an annual list of organizations that are highly regarded for the value they place on a multiculturalism.

If your child wants to take time off before entering the job market or graduate education, he or she may want to consider joining programs to benefit the African-American community.

"Less than 5% of African-American and Hispanic students living in poverty graduated from a four-year university. What are you going to do about it?"

Match Corps, a one-year service option in Boston

This program's purpose is to provide highly qualified college graduates to work intensely with four high school students for a year and contribute to their success. The *Boston Globe* has described MATCH as "a charter school that does itself proud demonstrating just what underprivileged minority kids can achieve." The Match Corps (www.matchschool.org) attracts students who are thinking about a future career in medicine, law, public policy, or teaching. Another short-term opportunity is the International Fellows Program (www.ifesh.org.), in which recent college graduates, especially Americans of African descent, spend nine months helping improve the lives of individuals in sub-Saharan Africa. The Princeton Review book *Best Entry-Level Jobs* recommends City Year (www.cityyear.org). Young adults spend a year in one of 17 locations—16 in the U.S. and in Johannesburg, South Africa—in community service. They also receive leadership training and make valuable networking contacts.

The African-American community has strong institutions that support the educational and career success of its youth. Chapters of 100 Black Men are located in many metropolitan areas, such as Chicago, Atlanta, Greater Washington, D.C., and London. This organization provides mentoring and scholarship programs, and offers collegiate chapters at some colleges. Twenty national organizations belong to Partners in the Campaign for African American Achievement, sponsored by the National Urban League. Some Campaign Partners include Blacks in Government, the Congressional Black Caucus Foundation, the National Pan-Hellenic Council, and The Congress of National Black Churches. The National Urban League also sponsors Young Professionals members and Employment Network. Fraternities and sororities provide excellent networking opportunities.

Asian-Americans

Asian-American students often excel in academics because of their strong work ethic and disciplined study habits. However, they may find themselves resented by other students who are not willing to devote as much time to their studies. Your child may feel a conflict between your expectations and the desire to be accepted by his or her peers. Graduate and professional schools and employers look at grades as only one criteria in admissions or hiring decisions. Leadership and teamwork skills are also important, which may be gained through campus activities or volunteer work.

Cultural differences can be misinterpreted by people in a position to evaluate your child. You may have taught your child to be agreeable and cooperative because these are highly valued qualities in your culture. However, students are expected to express and defend their opinions in many courses, and some faculty consider class participation as a factor in assigning grades.

In some Asian cultures, it is considered impolite to make direct eye contact with someone in a position of authority, such as a professor, college administrator, or campus interviewer. What is considered a sign of respect to Asian students may be perceived by job interviewers as indifference or a lack of sincere interest in a job. (In the workplace, Asians may stand out by their inability to address supervisors by first name, even when encouraged to do so.)

When asked about their strengths in an interview, Asian students may find it difficult to respond with confidence, believing that to do so would show a lack of humility. The job search process, however, is competitive and requires applicants to give examples to show how they are qualified for a position.

In a practice interview with her career counselor, Song Yi was asked about her strengths. There was a long period of silence, as she struggled to respond in a way consistent with her values. After talking with her counselor, Song Yi was able to answer the questions indirectly. Instead of talking about her high grades and many honors, Soon Yi responded that she finished her assignments quickly and was pleased to be able to help other students. Also, when no one in class answered the professor's question, he would call on her, because she often knew the answer.

Kim had worked since high school in the family business, a Chinese restaurant. Although she had earned excellent grades and demonstrated leadership in campus organizations, she was devastated to be rejected for employment by investment banks. The recruiters told her that she was not

245

competitive with students who had completed a finance-related internship in a large corporation. She had never questioned her family's expectation that she would be available to work with them during school breaks and summers. It is important for your child to obtain experience related to his or her career goals.

According to Asian-Nation (www.asian-nation.com), some medical professionals have experienced a "glass ceiling." Even though they have attended prestigious academic institutions and performed exceptionally on the job, they are passed over for leadership or policy-making roles. Because of cultural differences, Asians may not be recognized for their leadership abilities unless they are proactive in seeking opportunities to demonstrate their skills. Participation in a professional association can help members practice leadership skills and gain visibility in their field.

Hispanics

Students who are bilingual or fluent in Spanish have an advantage in competing for some types of jobs, such as marketing to approximately 39 million Latinos. For example, Kraft Food sponsors sweepstake events in Hispanic neighborhoods. Companies that have sought Spanish-speaking college students are Wells Fargo, the Bank of America, and Citigroup, among others.

The Hispanic Association of Colleges & Universities (HACU) includes 201 institutions. It offers an internship program; scholarships for attending the HACU annual conference and international study; and a student résumé database for employers targeting Hispanic students. The National Society for Hispanic Professionals (www.nshp.org/), works with student organizations, such as the Hispanic Business Students Association, the Society of Hispanic Engineers (SHPE), the Mexican American Engineers and Scientists (MAES), and Latino Association of Business Students (LABS).

GLBT Students

Many gay, lesbian, bisexual, and transgender (GLBT) students are just acknowledging and becoming comfortable with their sexual orientation when they are in college. The college environment is usually a safe one in which GLBT students can find campus groups, university departments, and non-discrimination policies to offer support and assistance. GLBT students are more uncertain about what they will encounter in the job search and the workplace. Some students do not feel free to discuss these concerns with their campus career counselor. However, an increasing number of colleges have trained staff and faculty to work with GLBT students. A program called SafeZone exists just for this purpose and is in use on a large number of campuses. Faculty and staff who have received SafeZone training typically display a SafeZone symbol in their offices to indicate that they are willing and committed to provide an atmosphere of acceptance and assistance to GLBT students. Students should seek the SafeZone symbol in a career counselor's office or inquire of the career services director if they do not observe the symbol.

A question frequently posed by GLBT students is whether or not they should reveal their sexual orientation on their résumé or in the interview process. This is a very individual decision, influenced by many factors such as the student's own comfort level with disclosure; the type of career field, industry, and particular organizations the student is targeting for an internship or full-time job; and the student's personal circumstances. There is no one answer that is right for every student. Some of the best material on this topic is available on the University of Pennsylvania Career Center's website:

www.vpul.upenn.edu/careerservices/wharton/LGBresources.htm

Students may very well want to join and become active in campus GLBT organizations. However, as with religious, minority, and political organizations, students should be careful about having all of their leadership and campus involvement with one type of organization unless they are sure that they want to pursue a career in organizations that relate to the particular cause. Advocacy organizations such as the Human Rights Campaign (www.hrc.org) offer internship programs and the Corporate Equality Index to help gays evaluate workplace environments.

International Students

International students have access to all of the services of the career office and should take advantage of them early in their college career. Students wanting to return to their home country will most likely have an easier time locating a job than those wishing to remain in the United States. Students seeking a job in the U.S. after graduation may face difficulty if they do not have a defined route to get a green card or to become a U.S. citizen. These students need particularly strong qualifications and are generally most successful if they are studying a field in which there is a shortage of workers, such as math or science teaching, pharmacy, nursing, other health fields, and some areas of engineering, computer science, or physical science. International students will generally not be eligible to work for U.S. government agencies - federal, state, or local - nor for any private employer that receives government contracts. Exceptions apply to some health-related careers.

International students should try to complete several internships or research experiences in their field by their senior year. When planning for an internship, they should allow a minimum of four months to petition for approval. It is often difficult to get approval for an internship that is not required as part of the student's curriculum. International students must stay in very close contact with their campus international office in order to be well informed about the immigration laws that apply to them regarding their student status and restrictions on their ability to work either while a student or upon graduation.

International students should seek help from the career office on writing their résumé, practicing their interview skills, and developing a job search strategy. While this is good advice for all students, it is particularly important for international students, especially those coming from countries in which these practices are quite different from the U.S. approach. International students can also benefit from training in business and dining etiquette, which may be offered by the career office. Again, students coming from a culture that is markedly different from the U.S. are in particular need of this assistance.

In some cases an international student may want to work on accent reduction if his or her English is difficult to understand. Some speech pathologists specialize in this service.

The career office may be able to help students locate employers who have hired international students in the past and who are open to consideration of students without permanent U.S. work authorization. Some offices subscribe to H1VisaJobs, a resource that lists jobs for students without permanent work authorization.

For international students considering further education in the U.S., the American Graduate Education website provides a description of graduate and professional degrees, the application process, and cultural information (www.americangraduateeducation.com.)

Students With Disabilities

Students with either a physical or learning disability should begin working with the career office, campus disability office, and state vocational rehabilitation office early in their college career to address their special needs and for advice and assistance with career preparation. They should inform the career office of any accommodation they require in order to meet with a career counselor or with an employer. Some employers such as Bender Consulting and IBM have special recruitment programs to offer people with disabilities the opportunity to explore careers with their organization. The career office may have a list of these employers on their website or in the office.

Students with disabilities may have questions about whether or not to disclose their disability to the employer on their résumé, before or during the interview, before or after a job offer, once they accept the job, or never. Disclosure depends on many factors, including whether the student needs an accommodation for the interview and whether the disability might affect the ability to perform the job. The Job Accommodation Network (a service of the U.S. Department of Labor's Office of Disability Employment Policy) gives this advice to job-hunters who have a disability:

"A cover letter …gives you your first opportunity to disclose your disability. This would be to your advantage if:

You are applying for a job with a state or federal agency that must comply with affirmative action policies;

The job you are applying for directly relates to your experience as a person with a disability such as a rehabilitation counselor or;

Having a disability is a qualification for the position."

Students with disabilities should consider the work they are interested in and capable of doing, prepare to be a well-qualified candidate for those positions, and concentrate on selling the employer on their strengths. There are numerous special internship programs for students with disabilities. Two of these programs, along with the employer sponsors,

249

are Emerging Leaders (A&E Television Networks, Exxon Mobil, Liz Claiborne, Microsoft, and Lockhead Martin) and Entry Point Program (IBM, NASA, Merck, NOAA, Google, and university science laboratories). Some excellent resources for parents of college students with disabilities are at :

www.washington.edu/doit/Resources/college_parent.html.

First Generation College Students

If your child is the first in your family to attend college we congratulate you on this significant achievement! While you may feel somewhat overwhelmed at the new environment your son or daughter will be entering, you are undoubtedly very proud of them. It is likely that they, too, recognize the sacrifices and support you have given them over the years to help them to reach this first family milestone.

Students who are the first member of their family to enroll in college face some unique challenges. Their parents may not be able to advise them about matters such as living in a residence hall, joining campus groups, choosing courses and a major, and preparing for careers that utilize their college education. However, perhaps there are other family members, or friends, high school teachers, ministers or rabbis that can help.

As a parent, we would advise you to pay particularly close attention to the recommendations in earlier chapters about students' early career preparation, the importance of internships, and frequent use of the career office. It is especially important for your child to attend all sessions of freshmen orientation, a program almost all colleges offer (and may require) to students before classes begin. Most colleges also offer a parents orientation program, which would be extremely valuable for you to attend.

You and your child should feel free to contact the career office staff (or any university faculty or staff member) with questions or concerns. Do not feel intimidated by the fact that you did not have the opportunity to experience college yourself. It is the job of university faculty and staff members to answer your questions as well as to help your son or daughter.

Females

....

Fortunately, things have changed greatly in the workforce, and women have equal opportunities to consider, compete for, and be hired for all jobs. Nevertheless, women often have added pressures and concerns about combining a career and family. Many career offices and campus Women's Centers have alumnae databases and special women's programming to allow female students to contact professional women for mentoring and role models.

Women's professional associations–both student chapters on campus such as the Women Business Student Association and the Society of Women Engineers, as well as local and national associations like American Association of University Women and the Association of Women in Science–can provide female students with support, role models, mentoring, networking, and career opportunities.

Resources

....

Minorities

DiversityInc.: Business from a People Perspective, Top 50 companies for diversity; www.diversityinc.com

The Multicultural Advantage (Career and Job Search Information for Minorities; includes Diversity Job Fair Datebook): www.multiculturaladvantage.com

Hire Diversity: hirediversity.com

African-Americans

National Urban League: Campaign for African-American Achievement, www.nul.org

BlackStudents.com (for students and parents): blackstudents.blacknews.com

The Black Collegian Online: www.black-collegian.com

Asian-Americans

Organization of Chinese Americans: Job bank, scholarships, internships; www.ocanatl.org

Asian-Nation: Doctors: The APA Dream Profession, The Model Minority Image, Asian Small Businesses; www.asian-nation.org

GoldSea: Best Careers for Bi-Lingual Asian Americans, 50 Great Employers for Asian Americans; goldsea.com/

Hispanics

Hispanic-Jobs.Com: hispanic-jobs.com

Bilingual-Jobs: www.bilingual-jobs.com

Partners in Hispanic Education: www.yesican.gov

American Indians

National Congress of American Indians: www.ncai.org

The American Indian College Fund: www.collegefund.org

Native Workplace : www.nativeworkplace.com/

GLBT Students

GayJob.Biz: www.gayjob.biz/index.cfm

ProGayJobs: www.progayjobs.com/

GLP Careers: www.glpcareers.com/

International Students

The International Student and Study Abroad Resource Center:
www.internationalstudent.com/

Visa Jobs: www.visajobs.com/

International Orientation Resources: www.iorworld.com/

Students With Disabilities

National Resource Center on AD/HD: www.help4adhd.org

Association on Higher Education and Disability: ahead.org/

National Center on Secondary Education and Transition
www.ncset.org/

First Generation Students

First in Family: www.whatkidscando.org

College is Possible: www.collegeispossible.org

Preparing Your Child for College: A Resource Book for Parents
www.ed.gov/pubs/Prepare/pt1.html

Females

Advancing Women Career Center (job postings)
careers.advancingwomen.com/home/index.cfm?site_id=299

Business Women's Network Directory of Women's Associations:
www.bwni.com/app_files/a_Search_Dir.cfm

Women for Hire: www.womenforhire.com/

Conversation Starters for Parents and Students

....

1. How do you think your particular situation will impact your job search?

2. What do you think are the advantages and disadvantages of your particular situation?

3. Which resources do you think will be expecially helpful to address your needs?

4. Have you discussed your special needs with a counselor in the career office?

JAN 2009

Printed in the United States
132076LV00006B/128/A

9 780615 163376